THIS YEAR I WILL...

BROADWAY BOOKS

New York

✦

THIS YEAR I WILL...

How to Finally Change a Habit,
Keep a Resolution, or
Make a Dream Come True

M. J. RYAN

BROADWAY

PUBLISHED BY BROADWAY BOOKS

Published in the United States by Broadway Books, an imprint of The Doubleday Broadway Publishing Group, a division of Random House, Inc., New York.
www.broadwaybooks.com

Book design by Gretchen Achilles

Library of Congress Cataloging-in-Publication Data
Ryan, M. J.
This year I will . . .: how to finally change a habit,
keep a resolution, or make a dream come true / M. J. Ryan.
p.   cm.
Includes index.
(alk. paper)
1. Habit breaking. 2. Behavior modification. I. Title.
BF337.B74R93   2006
158.1—dc22

2006015077

ISBN: 978-0-7679-2008-7

PRINTED IN THE UNITED STATES OF AMERICA

9   10   8

The biggest room in the world is the room for improvement.

CONTENTS

GETTING INTO ACTION
71

KEEPING GOING
149

TWELVE TIPS FOR KEEPING YOUR PROMISE TO YOURSELF
209

CONSCIOUS SELF-CREATION
217

THIS YEAR I WILL...

THE ADVENTURE OF LIVING YOUR DREAMS

We are what we repeatedly do. Excellence, then, is not an act,
but a habit.

—ARISTOTLE

"This year, I'm going to stop worrying so much."
"I will get in shape, once and for all."
"I'll stop spending beyond my means."
"I'll get along better with my family."
"I'll start that business I've always dreamed about."
"I'll begin volunteering in my community."
"I'll finally learn Spanish."

How many of us have made a resolution similar to one of these? We all
have something we want to change about ourselves or learn to do. Some

of us want to lose weight, become more organized, or quit smoking. Others want to tackle the more existential longings: a sense of purpose, more work/life balance, the courage to leave an unfulfilling career and start over. Whether it's New Year's Day, an important birthday, after a divorce, or just because we're fed up, at some point we vow to do that one thing we've always wanted—make that one leap we are afraid of or give up the thing that plagues us. But by the time the rosy blush of good intentions wears off, the resolution gets pushed aside. Not because we don't still long to have what it is we really want; but because we just don't know how to change.

I believe that people can change. Not just superficially, or temporarily. I believe that we have the ability within us to truly rearrange our inner landscape and make changes happen within ourselves and our lives. This is the cornerstone of all the books I have written and all the work I do with my clients: the awareness that we can stop doing the things that hold us back or cause us suffering and create a life filled with meaning, peace, and ultimately, happiness. We can make a dream come true or bring something new into being. Big or small, grandiose or humble, we *can* have the things we want in life.

But it's not easy, as anyone who has tried to change a habit or do something new knows. Our brains create strong tendencies to do the same thing over and over. We say we're going to change, we may even do it for a little while, but soon we find ourselves back to our old habits.

To bring new behavior into being takes *work*. Our brains have enormous "plasticity," meaning they can create new cells and pathways. But it takes certain mental preparation, particular awarenesses and attitudes, and lots of practice to create a pathway to the new options (six to nine months, say many brain scientists—so much for those seven-day-wonder programs).

Change requires that we stretch not only mentally, but emotionally and spiritually. It takes energy, determination, and aspiration, the ability to intentionally bring into being something we want. It requires starting over when we blow it or get discouraged. We may be forced to question our assumptions about what we're capable of, or confront our deepest fears. An acquaintance starting his own Internet business once told me, "My whole life I've been afraid of looking like a fool, afraid I've got a sign on my back reading 'Idiot.' But to get my business going, I'll have to keep talking to people who say my idea will never work and believe enough in myself and my concept to keep moving forward." When you go toward what you want in your life, you may find yourself in similarly challenging places.

To top it all off, what works for one person doesn't necessarily apply to another, so the advice you get from magazines, books, and the Internet may not be particularly useful for you. The good news, however, is that once you learn your particular success formula, once you've cultivated new inner and outer emotional, mental, and spiritual resources, you can apply those to anything you want to cultivate in yourself.

Do you keep hoping that a magic fairy will appear to make your dreams come true? That if you just read enough issues of *Shape* those thunder thighs will disappear? You're not alone. Most of us are not concrete enough about what we want, are unrealistic about what we can reasonably ask ourselves to learn, and don't know how to track our progress.

Here's what a new client of mine said he wanted to learn in three months: "to be less nitpicky and fearful; to be more optimistic, to be more responsible and empathetic; to be more creative; to be more productive; to live a healthier life and to take better care of myself." "How about create world peace while you're at it?" I replied. "And what does 'more' mean anyway? Even if it were possible to focus on all of this in that time frame, how will you know if you are more of any of these things?"

As this client so touchingly demonstrated, we expect too much of ourselves and we expect to change overnight. When that doesn't happen, we resign ourselves to staying the same, convinced that we are hopeless, weak, or unmotivated—which makes us even more stuck. As another of my client, eager to lose weight, puts it, "Once I eat the first cookie, I figure I might as well go through the whole box."

Social scientists tell us that when we change a habit or follow a dream we go through five stages: precontemplation, when we don't even know we need or want to change; contemplation, when we say to ourselves, "someday I'll do that"; preparation, when we are getting ready to do it "soon"; action, as in "I'm starting right now"; and maintenance, which means we keep going until we get where we want and stay there.

I've structured the book around these stages, beginning with preparing to change. I'm not here to convince you that you should overcome a bad habit or learn something new. I'm assuming you've already figured that out or else you wouldn't be picking up this book. (Although at the beginning of "Preparing to Change," I do offer a couple ways to choose which goal to focus on now.) *This Year I Will . . .* is meant to be a companion after you've made the leap to the contemplation stage and are looking for a hand to hold on to as you move forward. Perhaps you've attempted this resolution before and are worried about getting stuck again. Or maybe this is a change you have no idea how to bring into being. In either case, I want to help you increase the possibility of success.

Depending on what survey you're paying attention to, approximately 45 percent of us make New Year's resolutions, but only 8 percent succeed. Armed with the information and suggestions in this book, I know you can beat those odds. I've sifted through psychology, religion, philosophy, and brain science, as well as my experience with clients, to give you the very best advice on what actually works to get from point A to point B, no matter what your issue is. Rather than focusing on one resolution—stopping procrastination, controlling anger, finding a mate, losing weight, or getting out of debt, for instance—I will take you through the process of making whatever it is you want happen.

For the past fifteen years, as a writer and a thinking partner to executives, as a mother and a daughter, a sister, a friend, a wife, I have been consumed with understanding how and why people change. I've wanted to learn for myself so that I can be as effective as possible with the people whom I work with every day. What did I do to grow new habits of mind and body in myself? Where and when do I screw up?

Why do some folks I talk to make significant leaps while others stay stuck? My thinking about this was intensified recently when I read that 90 percent of heart patients don't stick to the lifestyle changes they need to make in order to live longer and healthier lives. Even faced with the dramatic choice to change or die, they can't do it. I don't believe they *want* to die. They just don't know how to make the choice for life.

I'm also motivated by the flood of bad advice I've seen out there. As I write, I'm staring at the cover of a women's magazine. It's the November 28 issue and the headline blares: YOU, 43 LBS SLIMMER BY CHRISTMAS! I'm sorry but you, no matter who you are, are not going to be 43 pounds slimmer in 28 days using their diet or anyone else's. Such irresponsible "advice" does a great deal of harm. Because it creates unrealistic expectations, it increases the probability we'll give up before we get where we want to go.

What I've come to understand is that there are three things needed to make any change, mental, emotional, or physical: desire, intent, and persistence. Each and every one of the ideas in this book strengthens one of those three elements. You will learn how to identify what you really desire; make specific, measurable, achievable goals to focus your intention; avoid common pitfalls that sap your desire and intent; and persist in the face of inevitable setbacks.

You'll learn that the process is not about getting rid of bad habits—the pathway to your current behavior is there for life, baby—but building new, more positive ones. Even stopping a bad habit, like smoking, is really about creating a good new habit, nonsmoking. And you'll discover that, because of the way our brains are structured, the most powerful thing you can do is to engage your emotional brain in a way that makes it easy, fun, new, and different.

Some of what you'll read will be familiar. It's included here because it works. Other ideas, particularly the cutting-edge brain science, will hopefully give you new perspectives and practices to try. And you won't find some usual advice, such as to reward yourself along the way. What's important is to find out what helps *you* keep momentum. For some folks that turns out to be rewards, for others it's something totally different. You will also encounter a bit of contradictory advice, such as take a tiny first step and give yourself a very big goal. Again, that's because each of us is unique. As I say in all of my books, take what works for you and let the rest go.

This is not an ordinary book that you read cover to cover and then put away. It's meant to be a companion to something you actually *do*. My hope is that after you read "Preparing to Change," you'll pick something specific to work on through the rest of the book. This means going through "Getting into Action," and trying out the ideas. And it may mean coming back to "Keeping Going," when you find yourself stuck or need to start over.

I'm passionate about *This Year I Will*... because, like my past books, it hits upon a very primal and definitive human need—how to cultivate new habits. When we have this invaluable tool in our arsenal, when we know that we can actually bring about the things we want through our own efforts, the world opens up to us in new ways. We be-

7

come empowered, and through our empowerment we experience greater satisfaction and fulfillment in our lives. We become the masters of our fate rather than the victims of old choices.

You'll hear from John, for instance, a client of mine who's lost thirty pounds in four months when he's never been able to stick to a diet before. His secret? Rather than seeing cutting out fried foods (his nemesis) as depriving himself of something, he's seeing it as a choice to feel good about himself physically and emotionally. He's incorporating one of the principles of change: "Remember What Will Truly Make You Happy."

You'll also meet Clea, who has been trying for years to complete her memoir and is finally writing every day rather than talking about writing. She did it by asking, "What's the Price of Not Changing?" You'll read about dozens of other folks who got more organized, lost weight, stopped smoking, found meaningful work, or developed greater work/life balance, to name but a few personal changes. It is my fondest hope that their stories will inspire you to take action on the things you want to make happen in your one and only precious lifetime.

TOP TEN RESOLUTION PITFALLS

1. Being vague about what you want

2. Not making a serious commitment

3. Procrastinating and excuse making—no time, wrong time, dog ate my homework

4. Being unwilling to go through the awkward phase

5. Not setting up a tracking and reminder system

6. Expecting perfection, falling into guilt, shame, regret

7. Trying to go it alone

8. Telling yourself self-limiting rut stories

9. Not having backup plans

10. Turning slip-ups to give-ups

Don't despair. If you read and follow the suggestions in this book, you'll be able to navigate past these danger zones and meet with success.

THIS IS YOUR LIFE CALLING

We have only this moment, sparkling like a star in our hand . . . and melting like a snowflake. Let us use it before it's too late.

—MARIE BEYNON

A carpenter decided to change careers. He had two children and his wife was expecting twins. They needed a larger house, and he needed a job that brought in more money. He went to his boss to explain. The boss was reluctant to see him go, as he was a very fine carpenter. But the carpenter was determined. Finally the boss asked if he would build just one more house. The carpenter agreed. And he did build the house. But preoccupied and distracted with his family and his future, he just went through the motions. He worked on autopilot and the house wasn't up to his usual standards.

Finally the day came when the house was done. The boss came to inspect. As the two stood at the doorway, the boss handed the carpenter the key. "This is my gift to you for all the fine work you've done over the years." The carpenter was in shock. If only he had known this was to be his house he would have paid better attention to what he was doing.

In many ways, we all live our lives like this carpenter building his last house—on automatic pilot. We go through the motions of our day without paying attention to what we're doing and end up living a less than stellar existence.

Scientists tell us that 90 percent of our daily lives is spent in routine. Such habit is a good thing. We don't have to think about *how* to brush our teeth or tie our shoes or make toast or drive a car. We learn it by practicing enough for the pathways in our brains to repeat the sequence without our "thinking" about it. That frees up our brains to do something more interesting and useful. At least in theory.

Habit is also a bad thing. Depending on what our habits are, they can become prisons of misery: habits of negative thinking, of self-destructive behavior, of patterns of inertia that are very hard to overcome. We've practiced those things over and over so they've become automatic too. And so now we are living in the shoddy house of our own making.

I find myself in the kitchen in front of the open refrigerator door with a piece of cheese in my hand. How did I get here? Suddenly my fingernails are chewed to nubs. Did someone sneak in the house and bite them? The tendency to keep doing what we already have done is very strong because the neurons in our brains that fire together wire together. Meaning that they tend to run the same sequence the next time, whether we want to or not. I love this quote of Edith Wharton that describes this trap so perfectly: "Habit is necessary; it is the habit of having habits, of turning a trail into a rut that must be incessantly fought against if one is to remain alive."

The brain's tendency to habituate means we go through much of life like sleepwalkers. That's why when we want to create new habits or change old ones, our most important ally is being awake to our experience. We've got to become aware of what we're doing or not doing. Throughout this book, there will be many suggestions for how to become and stay awake. But the first step is to truly see your life as the precious, limited time opportunity it actually is. You can make it a beautiful mansion. Here's how author Philip Adams puts it, "Most people can do extraordinary things if they have the confidence or take the risks. Yet most people don't. They sit in front of the telly and treat life as if it goes on forever."

I have a client in his early forties who dealt with a serious illness last year that incapacitated him for months. He came to work with me recently because, as he put it, "Getting sick made me realize that I've been sleepwalking through my life. I'm awake for the first time and I don't want to fall back into numbness again."

For Jessica Yadegaran, the wake-up call came in the form of a big birthday. A few months before she turned thirty, this reporter for the *Contra Costa Times* decided to compile a list of thirty things she wanted to do before the big day and write about for the paper. Her list ranged from things like learning to read baseball box scores and change her car's oil to learning to be more grateful and to ask a man out on a date (she's still working on that last one!). Reader response to her adventure in learning was tremendous. People from as far away as Australia wrote saying she'd inspired them to come up with their own list. "It makes me a little sad," she says, "that it takes something like a decade-busting birthday to make a change." Whatever it takes, I say. (You'll be hearing more about Jessica's adventures later in the book.)

Your wake-up call can come in many forms: getting fired; the message from your doctor that you are now obese; a milestone birthday; having to declare bankruptcy; reading an inspirational story of how someone started a bed-and-breakfast. However and wherever it arrives, consider your wake-up call a blessing. Your life, like my life, is finite. It will end, and none of us can say when. Do you want to die in the state you're in? With dreams unrealized? Negative habits firmly holding you back?

There's a Zen chant that goes:

Life is fleeting.
Gone, gone —

Awake.
Awake each one!
Don't waste this life!

Each of us holds the potential for our unique form of greatness. Whenever we bring something positive in ourselves into being, we come closer to living that greatness in all its dimensions. No matter what new habit or dream we choose to cultivate, we're also growing our souls. For the process of change itself teaches patience, humor, resolve, gratefulness, tenacity, and compassion for ourselves. These precious soul qualities alone are worth the effort.

You can achieve what you set out to. As Christopher Reeve, one of my heroes of greatness, reminds us: "So many of our dreams at first seem impossible, then they seem improbable, and then, when we summon the will, they soon become inevitable." In one of the last interviews he gave, he exhorted all of us to "Go Forward." May the example of his life and words inspire you as you begin this journey to your heart's desire.

PREPARING TO CHANGE

The moment one definitely commits oneself, then Providence moves too.

—GOETHE

One day you decide that this is it—you're going to get a great new job, lose thirty pounds, spend more quality time with your kids, finally get out of debt, learn to be more positive. For whatever reason, you've decided to get yourself in gear on behalf of something you want. Congratulations! You're at the starting point of an adventure of focused attention that will lead not only to one of your heart's desires, but to greater overall self awareness and effectiveness.

Before you just launch out there with great enthusiasm—joining an expensive gym, eating only tofu burgers, papering the Internet with your résumé—take some time to prepare. The reason? As Naomi Judd likes to say: prior preparation prevents poor performance.

This is a crucial first step that many people skip. But you will greatly increase your chances of success if you stop long enough to get clear on your motivation, understand why you've been doing what you're doing now, and learn a bit about what fosters and supports real transformation. Don't fear—you won't hang out here forever. Just long enough to read this section.

YOU'VE GOT TO REALLY WANT THIS

✦   ✦   ✦

One thing is clear to me . . . You can't do everything you'd like to do . . .
You must hold on to some things and let go of others. Learning to make
that choice is one of the big lessons of this life.

—REALLIVEPREACHER.COM

everal years ago, I read something about the scientifically proven
best way to do laundry. You're supposed to fill with water first, then
soap, then clothes. I'd been doing it backwards for almost fifty
years. I decided to start doing it right. It's now six years later and I have
never done it "correctly." Not even once! I always forget until I've already loaded the clothes and am pouring in the detergent. Oh yeah, I
think to myself, I was going to do it the other way.

My little laundry story reveals a couple things—first, how hard it is to
change a habit, even a small one. If I were really to change how I do
laundry, I'd need to post reminders on the washer. When I caught myself
doing it the old way, I'd stop, take the clothes out, and put the water in
first. I'd ask my husband to remind me as he saw me walking toward the

laundry room. Eventually, if I did it enough times, it would become my new routine. But frankly, I don't care enough to put in the effort.

That's the crucial point here—how important motivation is. Because it takes work, often a lot of work and sacrifice, you have to really *want* to bring something into being. Deeply, truly, honestly. Otherwise it's too easy to slide back into the same old, same old.

That's what's the problem with so many New Year's or birthday resolutions. There's nothing wrong with resolutions per se. In fact, resolving to do something can spur you into action. But in the glow of a fresh start, we make all kinds of promises to ourselves—I'm going to be kinder, spend more time with my friends, do yoga every day, take up the violin—that we don't really care enough about to actually do! Then we beat ourselves up for lacking discipline when we fail to do them.

Whenever I work with people who say they want to do something— find a man, change jobs, become more grateful, volunteer in their community—and they don't do it, I tell them it failed to pass the "I really, really want it" test. Because if you really want it, you'll keep at it. Despite setbacks, interruptions, and sidetracks. No matter how long you get off course, you'll eventually return—if you really want what you say you do. Oprah Winfrey comes to mind. Obviously, she really wants to drop her excess pounds. Because no matter how many times she's gotten off course and the weight's come back, she's gotten back on track and achieved her goal.

She's also the poster child for how difficult it can be. Despite all the help money can buy, she has struggled to make lasting change. That's why it's so important to only pick something that you really care about. Really wanting it creates and sustains momentum. And you're going to need that.

On the Prevention.com website, Joan Borysenko, Ph.D., encourages us to go beneath the surface to find what she calls our soul resolutions, which are "based on saying yes to your deepest longings . . . Goals rooted in what really matters are far easier to keep than facile resolutions that roll off the surface, right down the drain." She gives the example of making a resolution to lose ten pounds by June 1, something she failed at over and over. However, when she tapped into herself at the soul level, what came out was "I will care for my body so that I can continue to feel the pleasure of being fit and fully alive as I grow older." That was something she could really care about—and work toward!

What do *you* care enough about to apply the necessary elbow grease? Sure it would be great to have more patience with your kids, stop eating junk food, find a new job, or get out of debt. But what do you want badly enough to keep front and center in your life? To make sacrifices of time and energy for?

GETTING CLEAR ON WHAT YOU TRULY WANT

Not sure of what you really want to change? Here's a great practice from Dawna Markova, author of *The Smart Parenting Revolution*:

1. Write every goal you think you'd like to accomplish in the next twenty years. Write as fast as possible.

2. Then, write the number of years you want it to take (one, five, ten, or twenty).

3. Circle the top four one-year goals that you want the most.

4. Write down some of the things you may need to do that you don't want to in order to make these goals happen.

5. Choose the goal that you are willing to do the hard things for.

WHAT NEED IS BEING SERVED BY WHAT YOU'RE DOING NOW?

✦   ✦   ✦

Everything people say or do is ultimately rooted in the belief that these actions will lead them to happiness.

—TARO GOLD

llen was talking to me about wanting to stop her binge drinking. I asked her to pay attention to what was going on just before she went on a bender. Even though it was not an effective coping mechanism, drinking was her way of meeting some need. I wanted her to explore what that could be so we could devise other, more positive strategies. One day, she called me excitedly. "I figured it out. I drink when my life feels overwhelming or when I want to express my feelings but don't think I should. Drinking allows me to forget all my responsibilities. It also loosens my tongue so I get to say what I feel."

"How could you meet those needs in another way?" I asked. She wasn't sure so I offered a few suggestions. "How about the second you feel the urge to drink, you stop and go to your journal and write about how you are feeling? If you feel overwhelmed, make a list of what needs to get done so that it gets out of your head and onto paper where you can make a plan. If you're wishing you'd said something to someone else, immediately write them a letter in your journal. Later you can decide if you want to send it or if expressing it to yourself was enough." Ellen agreed, and so far these ideas, along with her determination, a twelve-step program, and supportive friends, have helped her stay sober.

Recently I was having lunch with my friend Sue Bender, author of *Plain and Simple*. It was she who reminded me that whatever we're doing, healthy or unhealthy, is always a solution to some problem. "In order to change," she said, "you have to ask what need the current behavior is addressing. Otherwise you may *want* to change, but not be able to."

This is a profound lesson. We do what we do because it serves some need. We developed a particular habit—of perfectionism, negativity, overeating, smoking pot, overworking, overspending, hiding, whatever it is—as the best way we know at the time to meet some need in ourselves. But because we're not conscious about what we're doing, *the strategy we choose to solve the problem eventually becomes a bigger problem than the original one.* The box at the end of this chapter offers some common examples.

So many change efforts fail because we bypass the crucial step of identifying the need being served. We can't make lasting change unless we recognize it and meet it some other way.

I first learned this for myself when I was attempting to control my anger. I kept "trying" not to blow my top. This trying would work for days or weeks. But eventually, I would have an outburst, followed by terrible shame and guilt. Then I'd promise myself never to do it again and the vicious cycle would repeat.

It was only when I decided my anger was serving a purpose that I began to get off the merry-go-round of destructive behavior. I began to see that I lost my temper when some unexpressed need of mine had not been met by my spouse, a need that I was too out of touch with myself to recognize. Blowing up after the fact was the best I could do to express my need. My work lay not in trying to control my anger, but in coming to believe it was reasonable to have wants and that it was okay to express them. The more I recognized and expressed my needs, the less I got mad, even when things didn't go my way.

None of us are doing what we're doing because we're bad people. We just don't yet know any other way to handle our fear, our loneliness, our need to say no, or to have solitude — whatever it is that's driving our current behavior.

What's the need that you're meeting by what you're doing now? When you find yourself doing something you want to change but don't, walk around and put the scene on instant replay in your mind. As if you were watching a video, see yourself doing the thing you say you don't want to do. See yourself eating a whole chocolate cake or being pessimistic, for instance. Whisper to the self in the video, "that's right, that's right." Then ask yourself, in a curious tone of voice, "What *is* right about this?" Just keep murmuring "that's right" in a lazy sort of way until what's right about what's wrong — the need being met by that particular behavior — becomes apparent to you.

For instance, when Tessa, a workaholic, asked herself what's right about the pace she keeps, she realized that she felt competent and successful at work and got lots of kudos for her achievements. At home, she was arguing a lot with her twelve-year-old daughter and feeling estranged from her husband. No wonder she stayed at the office! Her need to feel successful resulted in overworking so she wouldn't have to go home and feel incompetent. Once that became clear, she realized she'd have more success at home if she spent time with each family member doing something he or she loved. She began playing Scrabble with her daughter in the evenings and she and her husband decided to take weekly Spanish lessons together. Now she's feeling a bit more competent at home as well.

What need is being served by what you're currently doing? The answer will help you find healthier ways of meeting that same need now.

UNDERLYING NEED	"COPING" MECHANISM
To have support in figuring out your talents	Getting stoned to avoid thinking about it
To be loved, held, appreciated	Negativity, pessimism to "control" expectations
To have feelings received	Overeating as an attempt at self-soothing
To be recognized as mattering	Overwork to prove worth

To forgive yourself	Becoming perfectionistic to try and avoid mistakes
To avoid punishment or disapproval	Focusing solely on the needs of others so you don't take care of yourself by exercising
Rest and rejuvenation	Drinking alcohol to excess, "rewarding" yourself with fatty or sweet foods
Solitude and contemplation	Picking fights so you end up alone
Stability in chaos	Worrying as a way to feel in control
A sense of purpose	Overspending in an attempt to find meaning in material things

GET YOUR THREE BRAINS ON YOUR SIDE

✦   ✦   ✦

All human actions have one or more of these seven causes: chance, nature, compulsions, habit, reason, passion, desire.

—ARISTOTLE

"As you know, I've been working on walking away to cool off when I lose my temper with my kids," Cindi related on the phone to me the other day. "Recently I've been noticing that at the very moment I lose my cool, my head thinks, walk away, but my mouth is already giving it to them right between the eyes."

Ever find yourself like Cindi, thinking one thing and doing something altogether contradictory? Like thinking "I should not have another donut" and then scarfing one down? Or telling yourself "I should work on my project" and then turning the TV on? No, it's not just you. We're all a mass of contradictions, particularly when it comes to the things we think we "should" do. You know, those things you keep resolving to do but somehow never get going on. What's that all about?

Neurologist Paul MacLean says it's because inside our head are three brains, not one. Each corresponds to a different stage of evolution, and while they are connected to one another, each acts independently and is often at odds with the others. The oldest is the "reptilian" brain, which consists of the cerebellum and brain stem. This is the instinctive part of ourselves, the part in charge of our breathing, heartbeat, and all other body functions outside our conscious control. It simply repeats behaviors over and over, never adapting, never learning. Its goal is to preserve our life at all costs.

The second brain is the limbic system, which we share with other mammals. This is our emotional brain, concerned with feelings, instincts, eating, fighting, and sexual behavior. This is where we decide whether something is a good idea or not. The emotional brain isn't very smart. It understands "pleasant" or "painful," and "safety" or "danger," the patterns for which were created when we were very young. It propels us toward pleasure and away from pain. Whenever it senses danger, it sends the body into "fight or flight." Our muscles tighten, our blood vessels constrict, and our bodies are flooded with stress hormones as we prepare to fight, freeze, or run like hell. In women it releases another hormone, oxytocin, which gives us an alternative option: to tend our children and/or befriend other women.

The third brain is the neocortex, the thinking brain that distinguishes humans from animals. This is the part of our brain capable of reasoning. It's where abstraction, as well as spatial, artistic, verbal, and musical ability, resides.

So what does this have to do with keeping a resolution or bringing a dream of yours into being? Everything. The thinking brain is where we decide that we want to do something different. But depending on what it is, how it's presented, and what we've done in the past, our emotional brain may not cooperate. Remember what it's scanning for? Pleasure and safety. That's why we so often "sabotage" ourselves—our emotional brain overrides what our thinking brain has decided in favor of immediate pleasure or perceived safety.

If you are serious about succeeding with your resolution, this information is crucial. You've got to get your emotions on your side. We change not because it makes sense from the perspective of our thoughts (I should go to the gym), but by engaging our *feelings* (It's going to feel fabulous to be thinner). *If the change seems like it's too scary, too hard, or no fun, your emotional brain is going to work against it.* So what you're looking for is easy, fun, new, and different! Sounds like an advertisement, doesn't it? Madison Avenue knows what it's doing when it gets us to buy products.

Don't despair—I've taken this into account as one of the guiding principles behind all the suggestions in this book. For right now, ask yourself this question: What *could* be easy, fun, new, and different about creating this new habit of yours? What could be wonderful about having more work/life balance? (More time with friends? Ability to read those novels by your bedside?) Eliminating your credit card debt? (Greater peace of mind? A sense of freedom?) Finding a wonderful partner? (Feeling connected to someone? Having a person to enjoy things with?)

Hold the question lightly. Play with it. Your thinking brain loves to play, to chew over a question to which there is no immediate answer. Allow the power of your creative thinking (found on the right side of your neocortex) to percolate over the next few days. The more you can find what's fun and enjoyable about what you want, the more your emotional brain will cooperate.

YOU CAN HELP YOUR BRAIN GROW NEW PATHWAYS

Our current habits are like default settings in our brains—we've run the same sequence so many times that the connections fire automatically. Neurologists now claim you can use this capacity on behalf of your desired change. It's really simple. A few minutes a day, vividly picture the circuitry for the new behavior actually growing in your brain. Imagine new bridges being built that make it easy for you, for instance, to be optimistic or eat right, or take life in stride. Like imagining cancer cells being destroyed, this envisioning uses the capacity of the mind to physiologically create the images we focus on. You can actually create new circuits by thinking strongly about building them.

AMBIVALENCE IS NORMAL

✦　✦　✦

You don't have to be 100 percent committed, 51 percent is enough.

—ANTHONY M. GRANT and JANE GREENE

"There's a part of me that doesn't want to leave my cushy corporate job," revealed a friend who's been talking to me for a year about following his dream of starting his own business. "I get paid vacations, a 401(k), and health benefits. Am I doing the right thing by leaving all that?"

Sophie, approaching fifty, knows how he feels. She came to work with me because she'd been single for a long time and wanted to find a long-term relationship. She was going on lots of dates, but her modus operandi was, at the first hint of anything less than total devotion, to dump them before they could reject her. She'd just met a "divine" guy and wanted to do it differently this time. At least she thought she did. However, at the first sniff of rejection—he didn't text message her fast enough—she was back to wanting to write him off. When I suggested she hang in for a bit longer, she exclaimed, "Maybe this change thing is not such a good idea."

Anthony M. Grant is a coach/psychologist and an author of *It's Your Life, What Are You Going to Do with It?* In the book, he makes a very important point about change: "The most enduring state we find ourselves in at the beginning of the change process is ambivalence. We want to change and we don't. We want to get fit and we want to slob out. We want to end the relationship, and we want to stay where we are . . . This is completely normal, in fact almost inevitable. We don't know what the new behavior will mean."

We are ambivalent as we set out because we've never been exactly where we're heading so we can't know what it's going to be like when we get there. Will we really be happier in a relationship? Will getting organized truly make our lives easier? And then there's all that work it's going to take to accomplish our dream. It's one thing to say we want to lose eighty pounds; it's another to go through the sweat and tears to get there. It may require sacrifice—better work/life balance may mean giving up the big beautiful house for a more manageable condo or forgoing vacations and weekends to start a new business. Or we may have to face things we fear, like putting our heart on the line or getting attention for being thinner.

In addition, every single choice we make precludes another. We always give something up to get something else. It's natural to feel regret over the road not taken, even if it's a road paved with ten thousand donuts and another twenty pounds. As a quote I once read said, "Judge your success by what you had to give up in order to get it."

The point Grant makes about ambivalence is very important to understand because so many of us take it as a sign that we shouldn't go forward. Of course, it's important to look realistically at what kind of effort your resolution is going to take and figure out if you really have the desire to do it. But don't overvalue the nagging whispers to stay in the cozy corner of the-way-it-is-now. Remember, your emotional brain likes easy. As Grant says, you don't have to be 100 percent committed, only 51. When I challenged Sophie to assess which was stronger, the urge to run or the desire to stay, she proclaimed, "It's hard and scary, but I want to give it a try."

So if ambivalence is normal, what can we do to get over the hump and get into action? First, recognize that it's okay to feel ambivalent. Grant claims it tends to be strongest before you begin and decreases as you begin to see the benefits of what you've put into action. However, you may always feel regretful, at least a little. He quotes an ex-smoker now in great shape physically who, when asked how he was doing after a couple years, wryly complained, "Well, I have to admit the quality of my life has definitely gone down." Remember, it's okay to be sad about what you've given up or chosen not to do. All decisions have a price.

Second, be encouraged by this: when you do something new and challenging, your brain rewards you by releasing a feel-good hormone called dopamine into your bloodstream. And if it involves taking some kind of risk or chance, like performing in public or speaking your mind, you'll also get a boost of epinephrine, another feel-good chemical. So once you get into action, you are going to feel better, which will make the ambivalence decrease.

Third, read the next chapter, "What's the Price of Not Changing?" and do the practice I suggest. The more you see the costs of staying the same, the less you'll be stuck in ambivalence. By engaging more of your feelings toward wanting to change, you'll be able to get into motion.

By the way, it's seven months since Sophie had that crisis of ambivalence. She's still seeing the guy—"I'm head over heels in love," she told me yesterday. "I still have moments of wanting to run like hell. Not as many as in the beginning, though."

WHAT'S THE PRICE OF NOT CHANGING?

✦   ✦   ✦

Nothing can be changed until it is faced.

—JAMES BALDWIN

When I think of people I know who know how to change, my friend Barb comes immediately to mind. She's learned to eat well, exercise regularly, meditate every day, and have a wonderful relationship with her husband of thirty years. Recently she's committed to doing an esoteric Tibetan Buddhist practice that requires doing 100,000 full-body prostrations and chants. When she visits me, she goes off for hours to fulfill her promise. Recently we sat in my kitchen, talking about how she's been able to make these changes.

"The motivation comes first," she explains, "then the discipline. And for me, the motivation has always begun with my being incredibly stuck. I feel such physical or psychological pain that I simply *have* to make a change because the price of *not* is too high. I always start from a negative place. Inertia is really hard to overcome. But the pain finally builds up so much that I must take action. Once I get started, I experience such relief that even though it's difficult to do, I'm committed to keep going."

As I listened, I realized that Barb was talking about what alcoholics and addicts call hitting bottom—when you realize that the consequences of not changing are worse than whatever you have to go through to get to the new place. It's a powerful initiator because it engages the emotional brain's desire to move from pain to pleasure.

I've been in this spot more than once. The time that comes to mind is an embarrassing one. In an argument with my husband, I slammed down my dinner plate in front of my two-year-old. I was horrified. This was not the kind of wife and mother I wanted to be. My previous relationship had ended in part because of my temper. I had been given a second chance and here I was blowing it in exactly the same way!

Never again, I vowed to myself that night. And I'm proud to say I've kept my word. Not without work. I read everything I could about dealing with anger. (The best book? Thich Nhat Hanh's *Anger: Wisdom for Cooling the Flames*.) I practiced all kinds of techniques. What helped me the most was learning about amygdala hijacks, which is when our emotional brain feels so afraid that it wrests control of our thinking brain and sends us into fight or flight. In this state we end up doing or saying all kinds of things we regret later. I now know to walk away and cool down, no matter what. That's because it takes at least thirty minutes and up to twenty-four hours for the stress hormones to subside and our thinking brain to reengage.

If you've not had a hitting-the-bottom moment yet, ask yourself a difficult question: What's the price of not changing? Dying of a heart attack? An estrangement from your family? Forty more pounds? There are very real consequences to all of our actions. You can also take a personal inventory of what negative effects your current behavior has created (high blood pressure, boredom, shame, self-loathing, exhaustion). Have the courage to tell yourself the truth about the current and future consequences of your behavior. Do it not to beat yourself up, but to acknowledge to yourself that you're really ready to change.

If you've reached the painful place Barb speaks of, congratulations! You know you're at a dead end. And, Naomi Judd says, a dead end is just a good place to turn around.

WRITING A BOOK: "I DON'T WANT TO DIE WITH MY STORY STILL IN ME"

"I've been writing my memoir in fits and starts over the past fifteen years," admits Clea. "I've taken lots of workshops where I've read pieces of it and gotten very positive feedback. But somehow I kept getting distracted by the day to day of work. Months and even years went by without me even opening that file on my computer. Then one day, I woke early and realized that I am sixty-one years old. Unless I changed my ways, there was a very good chance that I would never finish. I realized that I don't want to die with my story still in me. That fear pushed me into action—I joined a writer's group so I have to produce something weekly, put my writing time in my calendar like it's an appointment with a client, and have now completed a second draft. I'm confident that it will actually see the light of day within a year."

RUN TOWARD, NOT AWAY FROM

✦　✦　✦

Our destiny changes with our thought; we shall become what we wish
to become, do what we wish to do, when our habitual thought corresponds with our desire.

—ORISON SWETT MARDEN

young woman called me up on the phone. She'd read my book *The
Happiness Makeover* and wanted to know if I could help her learn
to be easier on herself and others. I asked her the question I ask
every prospective client: "Why do you want to learn this?" Her reply was
instantaneous and clear: "Because I am getting married in six months.
I came from a supercritical family and have a tendency to harp on every
little thing my fiancé does. I want to give my marriage the very best start
I can."

Immediately I agreed to work with her. Because this soon-to-be
bride had a powerful positive motivation to change, she had a very good
chance of succeeding. Over the months, when she became discouraged
at how hard it was to transform her long-standing habit of criticism, I re-

minded her of why it was worth it. Making her relationship work mattered so much to her that it would reinspire her to keep going.

After a couple months, her efforts began to pay off. "It's getting easier," she exclaimed one day. "Even my boyfriend is commenting on how positive I'm being. And I'm not faking." She didn't do it perfectly, by any means, because she's human like the rest of us. But more and more there was a measurable tilt in the direction she wanted.

Like this young woman, in order to actually do something new, you have to get clear on why you are willing to expend all that energy. Why do you want to start that new hobby, have time alone with your spouse, get more sleep, move across the country, get out of debt? The benefits of where you're headed need to be clear. Just as you need a powerful what, you need a meaningful why. A strongly emotional why makes meaning out of the drudgery you may have to go through and gives you a reason to persist. In thinking about your why, muse on this: while you may have been pushed into action by hitting bottom, ultimately you need something *positive* that you want to go toward.

That's the insight from organizational consultant Robert Fritz, who's made it his life work to study conscious change. Fritz discovered that while we can motivate ourselves in the short run to make changes by scaring ourselves—I've got to stop smoking or I'll die; I've got to stop drinking or I'll lose my job—in the long run, we must be heading toward something positive we want to create: I want to live long enough to see my daughter's children; I want to be free from addiction; I want to make my dream of owning my own home come true. That's because, says Fritz, when we motivate ourselves positively, we are operating in the same way as the forces for creation in the natural world and thereby increase the possibility of success. Fritz is no New Age flake; his ideas are firmly rooted in the laws of physics. If you are interested in learning more, dip into his book *The Path of Least Resistance*.

Psychologists have discovered a similar thing. Trying consciously to remove a negative mental image or habit actually reinforces it. That's because if you give yourself a command such as "Don't think of donuts," there's actually a part of the brain that is trying to obey by constantly scanning ("Are you thinking about donuts now? How about now?"), which of course results in you constantly thinking about the very thing you've vowed not to. But if you create a positive image of what you want to go toward, that's what the brain begins scanning for instead.

Finding a positive motivation also engages your emotional brain to work for the change, not against it. Remember, it wants to go toward pleasure. So the more emotionally pleasurable your positive motivation, the more it will help you achieve your goal.

Give it a try. Find a positive motivation for why you want to make this change, one that engages your feelings: to feel better about myself, to make a meaningful contribution to the world, to have a healthier relationship with my spouse, to enjoy my life more, to be an inspiration to my children. Make sure that whatever it is, it has a positive emotional charge for you. If you can only think of a negative, write it down and challenge yourself to turn it around: Turn "I'm afraid if I don't find a better-paying job, I'll become a bag lady" into "I want a well-paying job so I will be financially secure."

And make sure it's your motivation, not your mother-in-law's, your spouse's, your child's, or your best friend's. Don't move forward until you've got a why that matters to *you*. Write it down and put it someplace where you can refer to it when you need it most.

RUNNING FROM	RUNNING TOWARD
Smoking	Health, longer life
Excess weight	Better-fitting clothes, greater self-confidence
Career rut	New opportunities, more money
Messy house	Being able to find things, sense of order
Debt	Sense of freedom and control
Stress	More relaxation, better sleep
Negativity	More joyfulness
Anger	Patience, serenity
Loneliness	A special someone to share life with
Passivity	Ability to speak up for what I want
Fear	Courage
Worry	Peace of mind

THE GAP BETWEEN WHERE YOU ARE
AND WHERE YOU WANT TO BE IS
A GOOD THING

✦　✦　✦

Dreams come a size too big so that we may grow into them.

—JOSIE BISSET

I was working with an executive, let's call him Jake, who wanted a bigger role in his firm, which was undergoing a huge reorganization. One day, he was complaining about his lack of recognition by his bosses and what was wrong with the company as a whole. So I challenged him to think about what he wanted, not what he didn't: "If you could do anything there, what would you want to do?" "Well, I'd really like to be marketing director," he admitted. "I've got lots of ideas about what needs to be done. But there's no way they would ever choose me. I have no background in marketing."

"Don't just assume that," I replied. "Just admit to yourself what you really want and you increase the chance of it occurring." I explained to him what I've learned about the physics of conscious creation from

Robert Fritz. "People tend to go into despair or give up when they become aware of the gap between what they want and where they are right now. But Fritz believes that space is a good thing. He calls it the tension for creation. According to the laws of physics, energy wants to move along the path of least resistance to the more stable state to resolve the tension. And the more stable state is what you want, not where you are now. For if you want it badly enough, what you want never changes, while current reality, where you are right now, is always changing."

"I do really want it. But how am I possibly going to make it happen?" Jake asked.

"I don't know," I replied. "But you don't have to, either. In fact, you can't possibly know in advance. You just take some actions, looking for the path of least resistance, and periodically evaluate whether you are getting closer."

Jake had his doubts but was willing to try. He and I brainstormed actions, including laying out a marketing plan in broad strokes and making the plan and his desire for the position known to the powers that be. We talked about who would be willing to champion him and how to recruit that person. A month later, he called. "You are not going to believe it. Tomorrow I will officially be named head of marketing!" I smiled.

It may seem like magic, but I've seen this process work too many times now not to believe. Put out what you want, tell yourself the truth about where you are, and get into action. Life will more than likely come along to help close the gap.

In *100 Ways to Motivate Yourself* I recently read about how Arnold Schwarzenegger used this exact technique. At the time he was a pumped-up bodybuilder with a heavy Austrian accent. He confessed to Steve Chandler, then a sportswriter: "I'm going to be the number-one box office star in all of Hollywood." Incredulous, Chandler asked how he was going to accomplish such a feat. "It's the same process I use in bodybuilding," he explained. "What you do is *create a vision* of who you want to be, and then live into that picture as if it were already true."

So if it's that simple, how come all of us don't get what we want all the time? One of the reasons, says Fritz, is that we don't really want something enough or don't believe we deserve it. So we get resigned to the gap between where we are and what we say we want. I once worked with a woman who said she wanted to change careers. We explored what she wanted, but it was all over the place. "I could do this, or this or this." When I challenged her to get into action, she always had an excuse: "This interferes with my exercise time; I don't want to have to go back to school; my biggest priority is time with my kids." I knew she was going to end up staying in her current job.

Your wanting is what sets the energy of creation into motion, drawing you toward your heart's desire. So you have to really allow yourself to want and to believe what you desire is possible, even if you don't know how. Fritz puts it this way: "If you limit your choices only to what seems possible or reasonable, you disconnect yourself from what you truly want, and all that is left is a compromise." So don't worry about how far you have to go—the force for creation is on your side!

CLEARING OUT CLUTTER: "DOES THIS LOOK LIKE IT BELONGS TO THE PERSON I WANT TO BE?"

"I had just divorced, moved to a different state with my three kids, and gotten all my stuff out of storage," says Jane. "It was the first time in years that all my belongings were in one location. I looked around at my small house crammed full of my possessions—Barbies and bride dolls and angels and dishes and clothes from decades ago—and thought to myself, Who is the person who has all this stuff? I wanted to free myself from the things that represented my past to make space for the person I wanted to become. So I resolved to go through every single thing I owned and ask one question: Does this look like it belongs to the person I want to be? I took it one category at a time. One evening would be dish night, another doll day. I put out five boxes: one for the eBay reseller; one for giving to friends; one for giving to charity; one for throwing away; and one for keeping. No matter how far I'd gotten, when I stopped for the day, I immediately put the boxes in my car and drove them to the appropriate spots so I couldn't reconsider. It took me about a month, but eventually I went through every single item in my house. Now when I buy something, I ask myself if it reflects who I am now. It really helped me move on after my divorce."

NO TIME IS THE PERFECT TIME TO BEGIN

✦   ✦   ✦

Every successful person I have heard of has done the best he could with
the conditions as he found them, and not waited until next year to be
better.

—E. W. HOWE

Trina has been out of work for five years. She can't focus on finding work, she says, because "there are too many other things
going on in my life." Over that time, her cat died, her boyfriend
broke up with her, her mom visited six times, a water pipe burst in her
apartment. . . . Her list goes on and on. No matter what's happening,
she always believes the timing isn't right to do what she claims she
wants to: find a meaningful job.

What Trina doesn't understand is that there never will be a perfect
time. Life goes on, with all its ups and downs. One of the tricks about
change is that we have to figure out how to do it in the midst of everything else. Fitness expert Dr. Pamela Peeke says, for instance, if you
want to get in shape and your mother is in the hospital, you've got to
find a way to walk around the hospital halls. In other words, you have

to make the change as much of a priority to yourself as the other things at the top of your to-do list. That's why it's so important to make sure this is something you really want to do. Usually no one is forcing us to make this change. We have to make it a priority to ourselves. Otherwise, it's too easy to let it slip to the bottom of your pile of obligations.

Recently I've been working with a high-powered executive who wants to change careers. She has an intense job, as well as a husband and children. Her daughter has just started middle school and needs a lot of attention. The corporation she works for is going through a downsizing and she has responsibility for a great deal of that. It's not "the right time" to be focusing on how to make a change. And indeed, she's let the idea slip for weeks at a time.

But she really wants to make the switch so she's committed to keeping the process alive. What has she done? She's following other advice you'll read about in this book—she created a specific goal (be out by November 1), focused on just the next step and not the whole thing (right now she's looking at credentialing programs in her new career choice), created a support network (she talks to me weekly and meets weekly over lunch with a friend at work who is making a similar change), and sees setbacks as opportunities for learning. But she wouldn't have gotten into action at all if she had told herself that there would be some better future point for getting started.

Naturally there are big exceptions to this—if you've got a broken ankle, this is not yet the time to take up running. And I just heard a study that it's much easier for women to stop smoking within ten days after the third day of their period than any other time of the month. Only 25 percent of women who stop then relapse compared to 75 percent who stop at other times (proving that there must be some relationship between cravings and hormones).

But for most of us most of the time, this is a totally unnecessary sticking point. I used to have a boyfriend in college who would set a deadline to begin studying: "I'll start at nine." The next time he looked at the clock, it would be 9:10. "Oops, I have to start on the hour. I'll begin at ten." And so forth. We used to laugh about it, but it was really just a procrastination technique. There was no magic about starting on the hour.

There's no magic either about starting on January 1, when your cousin's visit is over, or after you go on a binge this weekend. My friend Molly Fumia managed to write three books (so far) while raising six children. She did it by recognizing there was no perfect time to follow her dream of being a writer. Did she write *more* after the youngest was finally in school all day? Of course. But she got into motion before the conditions were ideal, which, given all she had to juggle vis-a-vis soccer, chicken pox, college visits, and so forth, is a state that has yet to come to pass.

Most likely this is not the perfect time for you to begin either. There *will* be obstacles. I often advise clients to consider these challenges as "do you really mean it" tests. In other words, do you care enough about getting fit, finding true love, stopping compulsive shopping, or being a Big Brother or Sister to do it despite the obstacles?

Peer into your heart and listen to the answer to that question. If you can truly say yes, then you can make it happen. As the old saying goes, "Where there is a will, there's a way."

STOPPING SMOKING:
"THE WRONG WEEK"

"Almost everyone remembers the hilarious line from the 1980 movie *Airplane!* when Lloyd Bridges' character, the head of flight control at the Chicago airport, complained during the worst airline crisis he had ever experienced that he picked the wrong week to quit smoking," says PR expert Suzanne Moccia. "As the danger increased throughout the movie, we also learned he picked the wrong week to stop sniffing glue, and to quit amphetamines. During the week of August 29, 2005, I was Lloyd Bridges. While the horrific scenes caused by Hurricane Katrina were being broadcast into my home, I lay on my couch with a nicotine patch on my arm, my stomach in knots, and tears streaming down my face. Three days before, I had finally decided to quit a thirty-year smoking habit. All I could say to myself was, 'I picked the wrong week.'

"The images of the evacuees from the New Orleans Convention Center yelling 'Help! Help! Help!' drove me to join my husband on the patio and take a few puffs off of a cigar, hoping to ease my pain. My lungs hurt and I quickly realized I could not cheat. Smoking would never make the pain I was feeling for the victims of the hurricane go away. I realized then I must never allow myself to have 'just one.' It's a fool's fantasy, for the grip of tobacco is so strong, I'd be slammed back to full addiction. So I went back on the couch, sobbing and praying for the victims and for myself. As of this writing, I am on day 340 of a completely smoke-free life. The worst part is definitely behind me. Early in the process, when I felt angry or sorry for myself, my catchphrase was 'Live with it!'—a reminder that this was a life-and-death decision. Would I have preferred to be able to smoke to calm my nerves and dull my emotions during those terrible weeks following Hurricane Katrina? Absolutely! But I realized the only right time was the moment I had already seized, so I ran with it, knowing it might have taken me a long time to pick another 'wrong week.' "

IMAGINE YOUR FUTURE POSITIVE SELF

✦　✦　✦

People get so in the habit of worry that if you save them from drowning
and put them on a bank to dry in the sun with hot chocolate and muffins
they wonder whether they are catching cold.

—JOHN JAY CHAPMAN

I take my wisdom wherever I can find it. Recently I heard about a
young man who dreamed about becoming a bull rider. The goal in
the ring is to stay on the bull for eight seconds. The first six months,
this guy worried constantly: "What if I get thrown right away? What if I
get trampled?" And sure enough, he kept getting thrown before the
eight seconds. Then one day, he decided to try something different. Instead of worrying about all that could go wrong, he'd worry about what
could go right: "What will I do with the wad of money I'll make? What
about all the fans who'll want my autograph?" He's now the United
States bull-riding champion.

As the bull rider discovered, when we imagine all the things that
could go wrong, we create a lot of internal interference, static in our
minds, that increases the likelihood of failure. Our emotional brains

want to move away from the possibility of pain, so intentionally or otherwise, we goof up or give up. When, on the other hand, we focus on all the positive outcomes, our emotional brain is attracted by the possibility of greater pleasure and so it aids in our going toward what we want.

Another reason this works is because, according to neuroscientists, we humans don't think in facts, but in frames. Frames are mind-sets that structure how we think. "We may be presented with facts," says George Lakoff, professor of cognitive science and linguistics at U.C. Berkeley, "but for us to make sense of them, they have to fit into what is already in the synapses of the brain. Otherwise facts go in and then they go right back out. They are not heard, or they are not accepted as facts." I think of frames as stories we tell ourselves about life that get confirmed over and over because we filter out any conflicting information.

How this relates to change is that each of us has a frame, a story about ourselves and life, that influences everything we think and do. Unless we change the frame, it will be hard to get different results in our lives. I know a woman whose mind-set is that men are not to be counted on. And guess what—her story keeps coming true. Is it because there are no reliable men? Of course not. But she interprets all behavior as proof that she's right, filtering out any time a man has been trustworthy.

Here's another example of how frames get in our way. I was working with Chris, who was probably forty pounds overweight. "I'm the heaviest I've ever been," he complained. "I've always been labeled the 'fat one' in my family. When I look at pictures of myself in my teens and twenties, I was probably a normal weight. But I come from a family of obsessively thin people. So my idea of myself is as huge. I never noticed this weight as it went on because the way I look now is actually the idea of myself I've always had." Chris literally ate his way into his frame of himself. Until he changed his story of himself, his weight would not go down.

One way to create a new frame is to do what the bull rider did—create a new, positive story about a future self. Then making the necessary changes becomes possible because you've got a new story to live into.

When Chris did this practice, his future self was a normal weight, neither as thin as the rest of his family nor as obese as today. Interestingly, the future self had a new name—Christopher. Christopher enjoyed walks with his wife and lower blood pressure and cholesterol. He'd taken up bike riding, something that Chris had loved but hadn't done since he was a teen. Energized by the image of Christopher, Chris got into action. Now, two years later, he's even considering entering a marathon!

Here's a "future self" letter from a woman whose resolution was to buy a house and move with a minimum of personal drama. She wrote this a day before her move. You'll see for yourself what wisdom the future self has to offer.

Dear Dina of Today,

Well, you managed to move to a new town without completely spiraling into your familiar "vortex of doom." I know it wasn't easy for you to stay optimistic and levelheaded in the midst of all the chaos and upheaval, but you did it. You learned to take your time making decisions, and as a result, you make far fewer bad purchases than you used to. You and your family are settled into a new routine and you don't feel compelled to fix every little detail!

You've learned a few other things about making this move easier for you:

1. *You've kept a personal, private space just for yourself with the things you immediately need at hand.*

2. *You don't immediately yell at Sam when things go wrong. It usually isn't his fault. You don't yell at other people, either. Workmen, repair people, and salespeople are much more likely to help you if you aren't shrieking at them.*

3. *You accept help from those who genuinely wish to help without an agenda—and politely decline help from those who offer it with an ulterior motive.*

4. *You remember that nothing is permanent. "This too shall pass" is a great mantra.*

YOUR FUTURE'S CALLING . . .

To create a new positive frame, write yourself a letter from your future. Imagine it's a year from now and that future self has accomplished what you want. The you of the future has lost the weight, become happier, found a new partner, learned to take life more easily. . . .

The future you is writing to the you of today about what it's like and how well you're doing. What does it feel like? What surprises have come your way as a result of the change? The future you is a year older and wiser. He or she has learned a lot about how to get from here to there. What message does he or she have to help the you of today get to that marvelous place?

UNDERSTANDING IS THE BOOBY PRIZE

✦   ✦   ✦

Don't ask why a person is the way he is, ask for what he would change.

—MILTON ERICKSON, M.D.

M y mother tells me my first word was "why." I believe her. I spent the first forty-five years of my life trying to unravel the mystery of why people are the way they are. I have a degree in psychology, have read tens of thousands of novels to understand the human psyche, and spent thousands of hours dissecting every person I've ever met as well as every friend of every friend I have. So why do I now say so often to my clients, as author Daphne Rose Kingma once told me, "Understanding is the booby prize"?

It is because I have finally become convinced that understanding why we are the way we are is not only not helpful, but can even prevent us from moving forward. Why can't I do this right? Why did this happen to me? Why do I always give up? We keep thinking if only we had the answer to such questions, we'd miraculously be free from the problem itself. But these questions are the type that, even if we have the answers to them, most often lead us into the dead end of despair. So what if you understand that it is because your mother toilet trained you at six months that your house is such an absolute mess that you can't even walk into certain rooms? Your house is still a wreck and you don't know what to do about it.

The tendency to get stuck in the whys (it's because I'm weak; it's because I'm adopted; it's because I'm too controlling) is so strong there's even a name for it: paralysis by analysis. It's usually used in the business world for individuals or teams who want to continue to gather more information in lieu of taking action. But it can happen to any of us when we are so focused on the whys of our current behavior that we can't get into motion to produce a different result. As Timothy D. Wilson wrote in a piece for the *New York Times* summing up the scientific research on the pitfalls of too much navel-gazing: "If we are dissatisfied with some aspect of our lives, one of the best approaches is to act like the person we want to be, rather than sitting around analyzing ourselves."

A bit of brain science may help here. When you ask why, you're engaging your analytic thinking, which is an activity of the left brain. Analytic thinking is focused on the present: the information that tells me why I am the way I am today. It is a data-gathering function, and boy, can it gather and arrange. Over the past forty years, I have gathered dozens of theories of why I am the way I am from all kinds of fascinating psychological and spiritual models. I have loved some and thrown out others. Some have given me great insight and comfort. Others seem petty or silly. I know one thing for sure—there is no end to them.

But to change something in myself, to bring something new into being, I need to engage a different part of my brain—my right brain, where innovative thinking happens. The right brain is future oriented. It's where our aspirations, our dreams, our longings reside. It's where creativity is born. This is the part of your brain that doesn't care that you haven't done it before—in fact it's energized by newness and bored by routine. It's the part of you that's excited that you're learning something new and wants to help discover the way forward. Innovative thinking is not interested in why, but in what could be possible. It's intrigued with questions such as: What do I want now? What's a compelling vision to strive toward? What do I need to do to bring my heart's desire into being?

In preparing for the change you're about to make, allow your right brain to help you. All it takes is switching from "why" thinking to "what could be possible" thinking. Ask "what" questions rather than "why" questions: "*What* can I do to have more balance in my life today?" rather than "*Why* am I a workaholic?" "*What* help do I need right now?" rather than "*Why* is this happening to me?" Do you notice the difference in the two choices? One leads to rumination and stuckness; the other to creative possibilities and forward momentum.

To reap the benefits of your innovative thinking and get into motion, you need to understand two things. First, the right side of the brain loves questions, not statements. So the more you can stay in questions, the more insight you will receive. You may also have to "hold" the question—meaning that the answer may not emerge instantly. But trust that it will.

Second, you need to know that the right brain is relational and metaphoric. That means the answer you get may not come in a straightforward manner. It may emerge in the form of a song you can't get out of your head, or a gut feeling. Or a compelling visual image. Trust that this is an answer.

Here's an example. Ted is drowning in papers that represent many possible business opportunities. He wants not only to get more organized, but to figure out which project to focus on. He's on the phone with me, coming up with all kinds of reasons why he can't clean his desk and choose one project over the other. I challenge him to let go of whys and try an experiment. Pick up each paper and imagine you're on your deathbed and you're looking back at your life. Would you be glad to have done this project? What would it have brought that matters to you? Then sort by your feelings of satisfaction and fulfillment. He did as I suggested and has now created a way forward to a meaningful career.

DEALING WITH STRESS: "I'M BREAKING THE HABIT OF 'OLD YELLER' "

"I had a lifelong habit of mishandling my stress," recounts Christine Hierlmaier Nelson, now a patience expert and author. "Having children brought my angry nature to the forefront. I had major baby blues after my first child was born and the dark thoughts really scared me. I didn't want to yell like my mother did or end up hurting my children physically or psychologically. Rather than getting stuck in why I had a temper problem, I began to try positive coping strategies, which have been so effective that I now teach them to others: taking a walk or going to a coffee shop alone for an hour to regroup; kissing my children when I was really frustrated (kissing increases serotonin, a feel-good hormone, and diffuses anger); empathizing with my children when they were hungry or tired rather than feeling they were out to get me; going to bed early at least one day a week and getting up an hour before the children to start the day in a more relaxed state; using meditation CDs to increase relaxation 'alpha' brainwaves; having a monthly date night with my spouse to reconnect and feel like a woman. My children rarely hear my 'grumpy mommy' voice these days and I am breaking the habit of 'Old Yeller.' When I know I'm stressed, I take time for myself now instead of lashing out."

BELIEVE YOU CAN DO IT

✦　✦　✦

People become really remarkable when they start thinking they can do things.
When they believe in themselves they have the first secret of success.

—NORMAN VINCENT PEALE

M y nine-year-old daughter and I were bike riding. I was telling
her that I was about to start this book so I would not be free on
the weekends for a while. "What's it called?" Ana asked.

"This Year I Will . . ." I said. "People will fill in the rest of the title
with what they want to do."

"Oh," she replied. "You mean like, believe in themselves?"

I was stunned. As she'd done many times before, Ana had gone right
to the heart of the matter. For no matter what habit or dream you are
looking to create, you can't do it without first somehow, somewhere inside you believing that you can.

The effect of self-confidence on achieving goals has been highly re-
searched—over six thousand studies since 1976. It has been found to be
a significant (and often the single most significant) factor in success in
relationships, work, musical performance, sports. . . . How come? Self-

confidence keeps the emotional brain out of fight-or-flight fear. And it's a reminder to our thinking brains that we can meet our goals.

So if self-confidence is a good thing to have, what do you do if it's not your strong suit? It's my perspective that we don't manufacture belief in ourselves by trying to talk ourselves into it. Rather, we need concrete evidence that we have "islands of competence," as Steve Jobs once referred to talents in a graduation speech. And the best place to find your islands of competences is in your past successes.

No matter who you are, no matter the circumstances of your life, you have talents and skills that have produced success. Even if you feel like you've messed up over and over, you have succeeded at something—finishing school, being a friend, painting a house, learning to cook—and you used qualities of heart and mind to do so. Perhaps you dismiss or ignore your competencies. But now it's time to inventory them in writing.

To create your competence inventory, select four to six accomplishments. Write down what you did. Then, look over your list of accomplishments and write down the strengths and skills you used repeatedly to create success. These are your competencies, the personal qualities you can apply to any goal.

Pull out your competency inventory when you are having a crisis of confidence to remind yourself of the qualities that allowed you to succeed in the past which you can use now. Here's an example. Cheri is a big worrier and wants to be more relaxed about her life. Her accomplishments— going to medical technician school while holding a full-time job; taking a trip to Europe; doing a 5K race; creating a small nest egg. Her strengths that cross all four include determination to succeed, independence, and courage. She decides to treat her desire to stop worrying as she did these more concrete tasks—she will remind herself that she can succeed, remember she can do it herself, and keep going even when she's scared.

Believing in yourself is built on the foundation of what you've already done in your life. If you have trouble remembering your accomplishments or tend to minimize your talents, find someone to help you.

You *can* succeed! Give yourself the energy boost of self-confidence.

WHEN IN DOUBT, TRY A LITTLE RAIN

This is a practice from Buddhist teacher James Baraz, to use when the self-doubt demons have you by the throat and you can't for the life of you drum up *any* belief in yourself. It's called RAIN: Recognize, Accept, Investigate, Nonidentify.

1. Recognize: Become aware of what is going on (Oh, here I am thinking I won't be able to do it).

2. Accept: Rather than "should"ing and shaming yourself, accept with kindness to yourself that this is what is going on (I'm afraid I will fail again).

3. Investigate: What feelings are in your body? What images come up for you? (I feel a tightness in my throat and an image of me lying drunk in the road comes to my mind).

4. Nonidentify: Tell yourself, These thoughts and feelings are not me. They are just passing through. I am more than these thoughts and feelings. I can choose not to respond.

WHAT IF YOU'VE BEEN DOWN THIS ROAD BEFORE?

✦   ✦   ✦

I have missed more than 9,000 shots in my career. I have lost almost 300 games. On twenty-six occasions I have been entrusted to take the game's winning shot . . . and missed. And I have failed over and over and over again in my life. And that's why I succeed.

—MICHAEL JORDAN

"I'm right back where I started," bemoaned Jan. "I keep trying to rein in my credit card debt but somehow it continues to creep up and up."

If you're reading this book there's a good chance that you've already tried, perhaps many times, to bring the change you want into being. You've lost fifteen pounds only to see them come back on, stopped smoking for months or even years (a friend of mine started again after seven years), done all the visioning work on what your next career should be but never got anywhere with it, started six novels. . . . You get the picture. How do you get off the merry-go-round of doing the same old thing again? How, oh how, can you have faith that this time it will be any different?

These are important questions. That's because if your emotional brain thinks the task is too much like what you've unsuccessfully tried before, it will sabotage your efforts. So the way to start discovering the answers is to recognize that you actually are not right back where you started. You now have a wealth of information and experience from the previous attempts, no matter how many those may be, to draw on this time. You know where you got stuck, what threw you off. But you can't access any of it if you don't understand that life is all about learning.

Carol Dweck is a professor of psychology at Stanford who studies why some people succeed and others fail. What she's discovered is that when young, people develop beliefs that organize their world and give meaning to their experiences. These mental models determine the goals we pursue and the ways we go about achieving those goals. She has found that the key mental models of successful individuals are: they love learning; they seek challenges and value effort; and they persist in the face of reasonable obstacles. She calls this having a *growth*, as opposed to a *fixed*, orientation to life.

When people with a fixed orientation fail at something, they believe the situation is out of their control and nothing can be done. They lose faith in their ability to perform. They shrink previous successes and inflate failures. Anxious about failure, they abandon the effective strategies they have in their repertoire. They give up.

Those with a growth orientation do not see failure as an indictment of their capacities. For those folks, a problem is just an opportunity to learn new things. Their attention is on finding strategies for learning. When they blow it, they realize that they just haven't found the right strategy yet. They wonder how they can improve their performance the next time. They dig in and make optimistic predictions: "The harder it gets, the harder I need to try. I need to remember what I already know about this. I'll get this soon."

Where do these orientations come from? It turns out that it has to do with whether you think intelligence is fixed (you're born as smart as you'll ever be) or changeable (you can get smarter throughout life). When provided with evidence that the brain can grow new pathways, fixed-orientation freshman college students on the verge of dropping out switched to a growth orientation and graduated.

Dweck's research offers powerful evidence that when it comes to making lasting change of any sort, it's crucial to adopt a growth orientation. Like those college students, no matter what you've believed in the past, please accept the scientific evidence that you are capable of becoming smarter and more effective. When we see our minds as capable of learning and life as a chance to grow, then everything we do is grist for the mill. We don't give up when we experience setbacks, but learn what we can from the experience and begin again, wiser.

Want further proof that success comes from accepting that you will make mistakes and you have the ability to learn from them? Would-be neurosurgeons were studied to determine who would succeed and who would fail. The researcher discovered that the answer came down to how they responded to the following two questions: Do you ever make mistakes? If so, what is the worst mistake you ever made? Those who flunked out claimed to never make mistakes or attributed any error to things beyond their control. Successful neurosurgical students admitted to many mistakes and described what they had learned about avoiding them in the future.

Like the successful students, if you have attempted this change before, think about what you could learn from your so-called failures that will help you now. Perhaps you fell off the wagon because you need a support group, or blew the diet over the holidays, so you know you need other strategies for special occasions. Take some time right now to mine your previous attempts for what you can learn about doing it better this time.

And take heart—the neuropathways you grew by practicing the new behaviors are still there. So starting over is at least a wee bit easier.

CREATING A GROWTH STORY

If this change is something you've tried before, it can help a lot to create what my colleague Dawna Markova calls "an integrated narrative," meaning a story about your past, present, and future that has a growth orientation. Most often we get mired in our past mistakes or our present stuckness when we think about a problem. When we add a positive future and connect past, present, and future, we give our brains a story that goes from beginning to end, which helps us create that positive outcome. You need: 1) an accurate description of the facts of the past, including what has and has not worked; 2) the facts of the present, including what you are learning that will lead to 3) a description of you in the future having achieved your goal. Here's an example. Tessa has been attempting to lose thirty pounds for a couple years. Her growth story could be:

- The past: I've tried several things such as smaller plates, which really helped, and strict diets, which have not.

- The present: I've cleared the junk food out of the house and I'm learning to notice when I'm eating too much.

- The future: Someday I will have no trouble eating just the right amount of the right foods.

YOU CAN'T GET FIT BY WATCHING OTHERS EXERCISE

✦　✦　✦

When all is said and done, a lot more is said than done.

—LOU HOLTZ

was on a panel discussing my book *The Happiness Makeover*. "What's the hardest piece of advice in it?" asked the moderator. I took the book and put it on my head. "To somehow take what's here and put it into your head. That takes doing. You can't become happier by reading about happiness." The audience nodded and laughed.

We're all experts at reading and talking about change and beginners at putting change into action. But as a Chinese proverb says, "Talk does not cook rice." You and I have all the advice we could ever need about how to find a relationship, follow your dream, spend quality time with your kids, get better organized, build positive attitudes. We've just got to do it.

In some ways, the flood of information from books and magazines and websites actually gets in our way. First, there's so much advice about what to do and how to do it that change can feel very overwhelming. Should you eliminate carbohydrates for life? Should you actively pursue a relationship or surrender to singlehood and then be surprised? Should you recite affirmations or do visualizations to bring something new into being? There are a million suggestions about how to do anything and you can really get lost.

Second, we confuse reading and thinking with doing. I'm as guilty as the next person. For over a decade, I've been reading and attending workshops on Buddhism. But do I ever put my butt on my cushion and actually meditate, one of the main actions of a Buddhist? Hardly ever.

It's easy to confuse contemplating with doing. I've had clients like this. They hire me to help them do something—become happier, achieve better work/life balance, discover what they want to do next in their lives. Then they proceed to talk to me every week about what they want, why they want it, and why they can't have it.

"Okay," I say. "What action are you willing to take this week to bring you closer to your goal? Here are my suggestions." They always agree to do something and then are back next time, not having done anything and ready to talk about it all over again.

I've come to see that the reason they are stuck is that they see talking to me as doing the work of changing. Our appointments make them feel like they *are* changing—or at least trying to. When you talk to a family member or friends about what you want, you too may be confusing those efforts with the actual work of change. As Montaigne reminds us, "Saying is one thing and doing is another."

Recently I heard this joke: There are five frogs on a log. One decides to jump off. How many are left? Five—because deciding isn't doing.

The hard reality is that we only bring something new into being in ourselves through action. Reading and talking to others can give us insight and support, and it can offer valuable reflection on what's working and what's not—but only if we are doing the heavy lifting in the first place. That's because the brain learns through *experiences*. You can't create new neural pathways by wishing you were different. Or talking about wanting to be different. Or reading about how to be different.

It's like the old joke about how to get to Carnegie Hall: practice, practice, practice. When you comfort yourself with a walk instead of reaching for a cigarette, a candy bar, or a drink; when you ask yourself, "what could be right about this?" instead of responding in your usual negative fashion; when you turn the computer off and turn to your spouse or child to have some quality time, that's when you are actually bringing the new options into being in your brain.

Research shows that for whatever reasons—sociological, psychological, or biological—more women than men tend to get stuck in thinking rather than getting into action. Whatever your gender, if you find yourself caught in overthinking this resolution, ask yourself, "Okay, now what am I going to *do* about it?"

There's another Chinese proverb that says, "Your teacher can open the door, but you must enter by yourself." It's time to stop thinking about doing and start doing.

GETTING INTO ACTION

A goal without an action plan is a daydream.

—NATHANIEL BRANDEN

This is the place where the rubber meets the road. You're going to begin practicing your healthy new habit or bringing your dream into reality. It doesn't matter when you start, only that you do. I have a client who thought about learning Tai Chi for seven years. When she began going with a neighbor she said to me, "This has been a long time coming. But I see now that I simply could not have done it alone." In this section, you'll learn the tricks that will enable you to get the most positive start possible: the importance of getting specific and concrete, tracking progress, enlisting support, finding the time, and cultivating the attitudes of a learner that will keep you from getting discouraged at your awkwardness.

As J. R. R. Tolkein writes in *The Fellowship of the Ring*, "It's the job that's never started that takes longest to finish." So let's get going!

FOCUS, PEOPLE

✦   ✦   ✦

Be like a postage stamp—stick to one thing till you get there.

—JOSH BILLINGS

When I talk to Marilyn, I think of a butterfly. She seems to flit from issue to issue. One week we're working on problems with her boss, the next week on her relationship with her husband, the following one on why she can't seem to find a cause to volunteer for, despite wanting to. "I don't feel like I'm getting anywhere!" she proclaimed on week four. I agreed. What she—and I—needed to do was to pick one change and hone in on that so that she could get somewhere.

When pundits look at why New Year's resolutions fail, one of the main reasons is that people try to change too much: I'm going to eat right, be more patient with the kids, learn to tango, and finish up all the household projects I promised I would do last year. They get emotionally swept up in the possibility of change that the new year promises only end up one to two months later in the same old spot—only worse, because they haven't accomplished anything but putting another failed attempt under their belts.

As Tim Gunn says in the TV show *Project Runway*, "Focus, people." Pick one thing, not seven. The emotional brain likes simple. Doing too much triggers the "let's give up and go back to our easy old habits" part of our brains.

Doing too much also doesn't provide the structure the thinking brain needs to focus on. New neural pathways are created through *repetition*. Making a new habit requires focus so that you can keep it front and center all the time until you no longer have to consciously think about it. If you're spread all over mentally, your neurons fire one sequence for eating healthily, another for being more patient, another for the tango, still another for closet cleaning—and none enough to make the behavior automatic. It's so much work that you drift back to same old, same old.

This doesn't mean you can't work on more than one thing. But your work needs some focus to constellate around, like feeling better by eating right and exercising more. Or becoming happier by cultivating the positive emotions of gratitude and optimism rather than worry and pessimism.

One great way to create such a focus that I learned from my sister Stephanie is to name the year: The Year of the Body; The Year of Learning to Say No; The Year of Household Projects. Stephanie's been doing this for decades every New Year's Eve. What she's doing is using the tendency of the neocortex to create frames, or stories, to make meaning of what otherwise would be random data and circumstances coming at us. We create these frames all the time unconsciously. But when we do it on purpose, we give our thinking something to crystallize around so that we increase the likelihood of actually doing what we intend.

The frame becomes a reminder and a motivator. If this is the Year of Household Projects, what am I going to do today to make that so? Once I do that, now what? It becomes like a North Star so we don't lose our way in the thousands of distractions and the busyness of our daily lives.

I'd like to encourage you to create a name for this time to focus your intention. It doesn't have to be a year. It could be a month. Or a week. It can be about something very specific—The Week of Liberation from Desserts—or something more general, as long as it has a cohesive theme: The Year of a More Positive Me. You don't need to know yet what steps you're going to take to get there. Just create a focus. Then read on.

GETTING OUT OF DEBT: "I JUST PUT MY MIND TO IT"

"I was single, in a big city, living paycheck to paycheck," explains Ed. "I had a student loan and a lot of credit card debt. My ten-year-old car started to die and I realized I couldn't afford a car payment. I was complaining to my roommate one evening, and he pointed out that perhaps I had no money because I ate out every single meal. I sat down and calculated that between my morning coffee and pastry, a sandwich and soda at noon, and a burrito or sushi in the evening, I was spending $17,000 out of my $40,000 annual paycheck on eating out! I realized that if I began eating at home, I would have enough money not only to afford a car payment, but to pay off my student loan in one year. I just put my mind to it. Not a great chef, I stocked my shelves with cereal and sandwich makings and my fridge with burgers and chicken. I cut up my credit card so I wouldn't be tempted to use it. Of course I ate out from time to time, but keeping focused on turning my financial situation around made it possible for me to become debt free. And I'm now the proud owner of a Prius that's half paid for."

ELEVATOR BROKEN, USE THE STAIRS

✦　✦　✦

The elevator to success is out of order. You'll have to use the stairs . . .
one step at a time.

—JOE GIRARD

My husband Don is a packrat. The only way I can stand to share a living space with him is that he has a whole room to himself for his stuff. Just peeking in there makes me nauseous. He's been collecting that stuff for most of his fifty years. Every so often, he complains about the chaos and disappears in there for hours. But I never see what I consider progress in organization going on. Fortunately I've learned to keep my eyes and mouth shut. (Well, mostly.)

Over the Christmas holidays this year, he decided to take charge of it once and for all. Again, he disappeared for hours. He finally came out and declared, "All that time and I could only find two things I'm willing to get rid of." I said nothing.

A week later, he pronounced, "I realize what the problem is. It's so out of control that it's overwhelming. I don't even know where to begin.

So I've decided that for my New Year's resolution, I'm going to throw away one thing a day. All I have to do is go in there every day and throw away one thing."

Smart man. He's figured out a secret to change: one tiny step at a time. And it often doesn't matter which small step. Just take one, as long as it's little. Then take another. Repeat until you've gotten where you want to be.

This is a great technique not only for clearing clutter, but for any task that feels overwhelming. What to lose fifty pounds? Concentrate on losing one by cutting out fried foods. (A male client of mine lost seventeen pounds by doing just that.) Or switch to light mayo. (A woman who lost forty-three pounds began that way.) The successes both met with that first small change allowed them to keep on going and up the ante to reach their goal.

Want to change careers? Take one class or read one book or have one conversation. Then figure out your next small step. Want to write a book? Commit to writing one line a day. Otherwise it can seem so daunting that you never begin.

It turns out that this technique has a name — *kaisen*, a Japanese strategy for change that relies on tiny, continuous improvements. It actually originated in the U.S. at the beginning of World War II and was introduced to Japan after the war. Why it works has to do with the brain structure I wrote of in "Preparing to Change." Whenever we initiate a change, even a positive one, we activate fear in our emotional brain. If the fear is big enough, the fight-to-flight response will go off and we'll run from what we're trying to do. The small steps in *kaisen* don't set off fight or flight, but rather keep us in the thinking brain, where we have access to our creativity and playfulness.

And when they say small, they mean *small*. Practitioners such as Robert Maurer give assignments such as flossing one tooth to someone who wants to create the flossing habit, or marching in place for one minute for a person who wants to learn to exercise. Want some scientific proof? Researchers at the University of Bristol divided seventy-eight people into two groups. One was told to take 10,000 steps per day, the other 2,500. Which group hit their target more often? The 2,500 group succeeded twice as often as the other one.

Breaking it down into small steps gives you the chance to experience success, which provides momentum to keep on going. It's also a great antidote to procrastination. You don't have to do it all, just one small thing. The other day, I heard Don saying to Ana, "I can't play cards with you until I go into my room and throw away two things because I skipped yesterday." The smallness of the task makes it possible to keep on going even when you mess up because it isn't a mountain of a screw-up. It took him all of two minutes to catch up. And with the daily small-step method, after only ten days his room is already looking better than it ever has.

What's the first small step to what you want? Go ahead—underwhelm yourself. The success you create will give you the courage and enthusiasm to persevere and perhaps even up the ante. Once you've done step one, put step two in place. As the great basketball coach John

Wooden once said, "When you improve a little each day, eventually big things occur . . . seek the small improvement one day at a time."

EXERCISING: "THROUGH SMALL STEPS I'VE BUILT UP MY ABILITY"

"For decades, I avoided exercise like the plague," says writer Susannah Seton. "Only when my back was in unignorable pain would I even venture a stretch. Then I hit fifty and middle-age spread finally caught up with my behind.

"The time had come to bite the bullet. I vowed to do thirty minutes of exercise three times a week. I joined a circuit training place that promised cardio and strengthening in one set routine. I couldn't even cheat—no switching to the next station until the recorded voice said so. I did that for a year. The next year, having mostly kept my promise to myself, I upped the ante—thirty minutes *every* day. Again, I mostly succeeded (about 75–80 percent of the time). So this year, I've again pledged thirty minutes a day but have now joined a gym with a much wider variety of equipment to track fitness levels, heart rate, etc. If I'd tried to go every day to this macho gym at the very beginning, I wouldn't have lasted a week. But through small steps, I've built up my ability and confidence to hang in there with the real athletes."

CREATE A HUGE CHALLENGE
FOR YOURSELF

✦   ✦   ✦

I hope to remind people like me that we each have the strength and ability to do anything we want. Losing weight is a choice the same as con-
tinuing to exist in this terrible condition is a choice. I have decided to
live! It really is a simple decision when you think about it.

—STEVE VAUGHT

A few months before he turned forty, 410-pound Steve Vaught was
struck by a jolt of reality: if he didn't lose a *lot* of weight, he
wouldn't live to see fifty. Being a "happily married father of two
great kids," as he describes himself in his online journal, this was not a
future he wanted to resign himself to. No diet or exercise plan had
worked, he explained, because he was good at rationalization. Very
good. So he decided, in his words, to create "rehab for the fat guy" by
taking six months to walk across the United States from his hometown
of San Diego to New York City.

As I write, it is just shy of one year to the day since he set out. He's
in Wheeling, West Virginia, having walked 2,409 miles. It's taken longer

for a variety of reasons, including a knee injury and stress fractures. He's lost over 100 pounds and gained a tremendous amount of insight: "Losing 102 lbs is significant and important," he writes, "but dwelling on a number or becoming a slave to a scale is a surefire way to fail at weight loss. I have learned to judge my health not by a scale of weight but by a scale of mental harmony. Once you accept that you are in control of your life and weight . . . and work on curing the emotional base of the weight problem you will find that the body will take care of itself . . . In short—Cure the mind and the ass will follow!"

Steve's intuitively setting a really high bar for himself jibes with certain research that shows that dramatic changes may be more effective than small ones. Heart patients following Dean Ornish's strict low-fat diet, for instance, had greater success sustaining their diet and exercise regimens over time than those advised to take a more moderate approach. Researchers speculate it is because with a drastic change, you get quicker results and therefore are rewarded by feeling better, which inspires you to keep on going.

I wonder whether a big change approach works better in certain situations than others. Namely, ones in which it really is a matter of life or death. Bypass surgery folks, those who've had heart attacks, folks with serious chemical addictions, and obese men and women like Steve— they must change or die. It's that simple. Half measures are just not going to cut it in those circumstances. That's a very different circumstance than wanting to learn to ride a Harley-Davidson or take a solo vacation. In those non–life-or-death situations, a small-step approach might serve better.

I also wonder whether different folks do better with one approach or the other, depending on their personalities and talents. I haven't come across any research on this. But I would guess that some people really do well with a big kick-in-the-pants goal, while others are instantly de-motivated by the enormity of the task. For instance, a client who vowed to work out twenty minutes three times a week had no success. "It's so small it's easy for me to blow off," she explained. When she upped it to an hour three times a week, she had better results. For me, just think-ing about doing a solid hour makes me nauseous. I had more success when I began with thirty minutes three times a week.

Not sure which approach to try? Read the next chapter, "Follow Your Formula for Success." You may find clues there. If not, pick one approach and try it in the spirit of experimentation and then switch if it isn't working. And if you'd like a dose of inspiration, go to www.thefat manwalking.com to read more about Steve's adventure.

TURNING YOUR WHOLE LIFE AROUND:
"AM I LIVING THE LIFE THAT WANTS TO LIVE IN ME?"

"I was at a retreat when the leader, Dawna Markova, asked that life-altering question," explained Holly. "Am I living the life that wants to live in me? Immediately the answer came back strongly: no. I was over-weight, a smoker, never exercised, in a relationship that was going nowhere, in a job and city I hated, surrounded by people just like me. I'm

very people oriented. I realized I needed to be in a healthier environment where everyone else was into exercising and eating right so that
I would have no one to hang out with if I didn't change my ways. Connecting to the environment that inspired me and listening to my intu-
ition, I turned my whole life upside down. I pulled up stakes and moved
to Park City, Utah. I stopped smoking and now work out daily, eat better, meet friends for a hike instead of at a bar. I've got a job I love
and have learned a whole new way of interfacing socially—this is a
place where people BYOP (Bring Your Own Protein) to parties. Now,
five years later, I'm so glad I took the leap of faith to turn my life around.
My good habits are just that—habits. I may backslide sometimes, but I
know how to get into positive motion again quickly."

FOLLOW YOUR FORMULA FOR SUCCESS

✦ ✦ ✦

The ark was built by amateurs and the *Titanic* by experts.
Don't wait for experts.

—MURRAY COHEN

recently read that when singer/songwriter Billy Joel is struggling with writer's block, he doesn't go to a shrink or a song doctor. Rather he puts on the clothes he's worn when he's written in the past, goes to the café where he's written well before, orders the same drink, and uses the same pen and notebook that have brought him success in the past.

How have you changed a habit or learned something new in the past? That is a crucial question to consider as you set out this time. Unfortunately we so often cut ourselves off from the resource of our past successes because of the capacity of the mind to compartmentalize, meaning we wall off one experience from another: *that* was about learning tennis and *this* is about feeding my family healthier meals. They are in such different categories that we don't even wonder what success in one could possibly have to do with succeeding at the other.

We also don't follow our formula for past successes because we get too caught up in looking outside ourselves for the answers. Instead of mining your own inner resources when you want to learn how to quilt, for instance, you do what worked for Aunt Tilly. Or you do what you just read in *Cosmo* when you want to have a better sex life. There's no dearth of experts telling us how and when and where to do every conceivable thing. That leads us to try someone else's recipe for success rather than follow our own. Many of us are so focused on advice outside of ourselves that we don't even know what our particular success formula is.

This is a big problem. For our past successes are treasure troves for creating success this time around. Knowing your formula can help you figure out the steps to take and the pitfalls to avoid. And best news of all, you'll learn faster this time because it's much easier for the brain to take something it already knows how to do and apply it to a new circumstance than it is to create a whole new pathway.

To apply your success formula requires letting down the little walls in your mind between one thing and another, and believing that you are your own best expert. Are you willing to give it a try? Start by thinking about anything in the past that you were motivated to learn and you did. Then think about *how* you did it. Take another one, then another. Does a pattern emerge?

For instance, I've learned to be much more grateful. I did it by first reading what others had written to inspire me, then creating two very simple practices to do on a daily basis (thanks before dinner with my family and reminding myself of what I was grateful for every time I started to worry about anything). In looking at other habits I've created,

I realize I did the exact same thing to learn to be more generous and patient, to be less angry, even to get fit. I read for inspiration, then I create one or two practices and do them.

In looking over my pattern, I realize something else. Part of my formula for success is that once I pick a practice, I stick to it. I'm still doing all the practices I put in place for anger, generosity, gratitude, patience, and exercise. I don't switch to something else, I don't ask myself whether I feel like doing it. I just keep plodding on with what I committed to. Come to think of it, that's also how I've written all the books I have. I read everything on the subject, then sit at the computer day after day. I don't ask myself if I want to get up on Saturday and go to the computer. Of course I don't. I just do it.

Now don't get excited and think that you've discovered the secret to success. That's *mine*. I know people who hate routine, whose formula for success is to mix it up, doing lots of different things so they don't get bored. I know people who never read to begin with, who jump in and adjust as they go along. I know folks who first need to research and buy all the best equipment.

The point is for you to discover your own formula so you can use it now. In thinking back on past successes, *how* did you go about learning something? Ask a loving friend or family member to help if you're having trouble seeing the pattern. Once you've found it, what does that mean for the steps you're going to take for this new habit?

STRONGLY SET YOUR INTENTION

✦　✦　✦

The truth is that, no matter what kind of game you find yourself in, no matter how good or bad the luck, you can change your life completely with a single thought.

—DAVID GREGORY ROBERTS

My friend Linda has had serious health problems for the past six years that have left her with limited energy and ability to engage with life. She's determined to get healthier this year. "I recently became aware of how powerful a positive intention is," she explained to me. "I strongly believe that we bring into being what we persistently focus on. When you don't feel well, it's easy to spiral down into worry that you never will be well and inadvertently focus on that. So I consciously use a daily intention to keep my focus on what I want, not what I don't.

"Here's what I do. When I wake in the morning, regardless of how I'm feeling, I look for what does feel good. Rather than focusing on my head hurting, for instance, I focus on the fact that my legs are working well. Then I remind myself that my intention is to feel good today. As I go through the day making choices, I ask myself, Will this food make me feel good? Will this exercise make me feel good? Will this conversation make me feel good?

I love Linda's approach. It's a very powerful yet simple way to use intention like the North Star, a way to notice where you already have some of what you want and orient through the day to get more of it.

I began to suggest her approach to clients. To the woman who wanted more peace, I suggested she notice with gratitude the peace she is already experiencing, set her intention for peace during the day, and ask herself at choice points whether the action before her would bring her more peace. When she got an annoying e-mail from a coworker or a demanding call from her mother about a family event on the weekend, she'd asked herself, What response would bring me the greatest peace? This allowed her to let things go that she would normally have gotten upset about and to respond in more thoughtful ways to coworkers and family members.

To the man who wanted to be thinner, I suggested that first thing in the morning, he should stop and notice when he's eaten right so far, set his intention to eat well that day, and then make choices accordingly. Will eating this help me with my intention to be thinner? he now asks before putting anything into his mouth.

What both clients discovered was that this simple practice made it easier to get to where they wanted to go. That's because one of our greatest allies of transformation is intention—the drive to do something different. Intention is not wanting, wishing, or hoping; it's the determination to do. Intention allows us not to be prisoners of the past, but to shape a better future by the thoughts we hold in the present. With intention, we indicate to ourselves that we are going to do something no matter what. And by noticing where and when we've already gotten what we intend to, we recognize that what we're looking for already exists in us. It's a matter of focusing our intention so that it can grow even stronger and taking the actions that make our intention turn into reality.

One powerful way to signal intention as we set out is to create some kind of ritual to mark our commitment. This is particularly useful if we've tried to make this change before. For instance, Joan had been a smoker for more than twenty years. She'd quit for brief periods of time. But she knew that she was stopping for good the day she and two friends decided to do a smoking funeral. They went to a hillside and smoked for a final time. Then they buried their cigarettes and matches and declared their intention to live cigarette free.

It's been almost twenty years since that day and Joan has never touched another cigarette. I believe her ceremony helped a lot. Here's why. When we declare, "I'm going to do this (live more simply, find a life partner, put myself on my to-do list) and back it up with some kind of ceremony, we engage all of our brain on behalf of what we want. Stating an intention is a left-brained activity. It's logical and analytic. Expressing that same intention in a ceremony engages our right brain, where images and symbols reside. With both sides activated, we're more likely to succeed.

The ceremony doesn't have to be elaborate. It can be as simple as writing down what you are letting go of and then burning up the paper. Or finding a heart-shaped stone that represents your intention to take good care of yourself and finding a special place to display it. Think about whether you would like someone else present. The presence of witnesses, like at a wedding, help confirm that you really mean it.

Draw on the power of intention to help you succeed. As Abraham Lincoln, who lost elections over and over before coming president, once said: "Always bear in mind that your own resolution to success is more important than any other one thing."

INCREASING SELF-ESTEEM:
"LIKING MYSELF BETTER TOMORROW"

"I've been working with a personal trainer, who's really helped me get in better shape physically," said Michael. "But mentally I'm still very down on myself. He, however, is always so upbeat. One day I asked him what his secret was. He told me that before he goes to sleep, he asks himself, 'How can I live so that tomorrow is a great day?' It helps him focus on what he truly wants. Inspired by him, I began telling myself that it is my intention to like myself better tomorrow. It helps me to wake up in a more positive frame of mind and to take actions that make that intention true. At night, I review the day and again set my intention. Even my wife's noticed a difference in the way I'm thinking about myself."

CREATE A **SMART** GOAL

✦   ✦   ✦

Goals are dreams with deadlines.

—DIANA SCHARF HUNT

lice, a busy magazine executive I know, recently decided to learn
to play the guitar. "At first I got hung up on the fact that I don't
have seven hours a week to devote to practice," she explained,
"and would therefore never be as great as I wanted to be. But I decided
not to worry about that and decided to take a weekly one-hour lesson for
six months and practice fifteen minutes a day. I'm really enjoying it!"

Alice understands intuitively the best thing I ever learned about
helping individuals and organizations change: you must create goals
that are SMART: SPECIFIC, MEASURABLE, ACHIEVABLE, RELEVANT, and
TIME-BOUND. Without these five elements, success can be very elusive.

SPECIFIC refers to choosing something that you can pin down.
"Learning the guitar" is specific; you know what you need to do to. "Becoming a better person" is not. What do you mean by that? How will
you know if you've done it? When we create a vague goal, we set ourselves up for failure. Because we're never quite sure when we've crossed

the finish line. So be sure to create something as specific as possible—
for instance, "Learn how to say no" rather than "get better boundaries"
or "Take one weekend day every month to myself" rather than "make
time for myself."

MEASURABLE means just that—capable of being measured. People
come to me all the time wanting "more": "more patience," "more
time with kids," "more happiness." I always say in response, "as measured by what?" Measurement is crucial because it makes our progress
visible to us. Without it, it's easy to feel like you haven't gotten anywhere or to exaggerate in your own mind how far you've come. If your
goal is to stop smoking, or lose twenty pounds, that's easy to measure.
But it is possible to create a measurement for anything. I've just
worked with a client to create a measure for finding a new relationship. He's going to track the number of conversations with new
women per week.

In thinking about measurement, it helps to understand that it can
be external (pounds, dollars, days, lower blood pressure, etc.) or internal (a sense of inner ease or peace, greater energy or excitement). The
numbers for the first category are obvious. When you're measuring
something internal, you need to put it on a scale, for instance -5 to +5,
with -5 being the worst you ever felt and +5 being the best.

Let me give you an example. Imagine that you want to be able to be
more tolerant of your in-laws. First you'd notice what your exasperation
number is right now, before you learn anything new. Maybe it's a lot,
say -4. You decide that your measure of success will be getting that num-

ber to +3, feeling much more calm in your body. That way you'll know when you can declare success—when you've gotten to +3 when around your in-laws.

ACHIEVABLE means being realistic about what's possible. Despite what magazine tabloids promise, you're not going to lose twenty-five pounds in a week. Don't set yourself up for failure by trying something that's just not possible. Look at your life and decide what you can reasonably do. That's what Alice did so well. She knows that in her work circumstances, she's not about to become a concert-level player. So she set a more achievable goal—to learn the guitar well enough to enjoy herself.

RELEVANT means something that matters to you. As we saw in "Preparing to Change," if you don't have a really good reason for doing this thing, it's too easy to drop it. You've got to know why it's important to you.

TIME-BOUND refers to creating a time in the future when you will be "done." Alice is going to take lessons for six months. Having an endpoint puts a structure around what you're doing. It allows you to have something to aim for. Even if this is something you're planning on doing forever, it often helps to put a time boundary around it so that it doesn't feel so overwhelming. Then when you get to the "end," you can sign on again if need be.

When you create a SMART goal, you know when you've arrived, which is crucial to creating a sense of satisfaction and completion. Without that sense of completion, it's easy to stay in a perpetual state of dissatisfaction with yourself. This is dangerous because it not only obliterates your actual success but discourages your emotional brain from ever trying to learn anything else. Conversely, when you set a SMART goal and achieve it, you not only experience the joy of a job well done, you reinforce your ability to tackle something else.

For practice, look at the difference between two genuine New Year's resolutions I recently heard. Jeff's is "to lose 1½ pounds each month by the year's end." Mort's is "to spend more quality time with my wife, without the kids." Whose is SMART? Jeff's. His is specific, measured by a scale, achievable (experts say you can lose one to two pounds per week, so within a month it is certainly doable), relevant (he's refereeing his daughter's soccer matches and wants to be able to run around easily), and time-bound. Conversely, if Mort truly wants to enact his resolution, he needs to do some work around getting more specific and measurable.

Stanford professor Carol Dweck discovered something similar when she looked at the difference between those with a growth versus a fixed orientation. When "growth" folks made plans, they included what, where, how, and when in their thinking. "Fixed" orientation planners went on willpower, saying, "I'm just going to do it." Guess which group was more successful?

It's time for you to create a SMART goal. Like Jeff's, it should be specific, have a measurement technique and time, be achievable and extremely relevant to you, and have an endpoint. From here on out, we're going to look at how to make this SMART goal happen.

USING YOUR SMARTS

Here's an example of turning the desire for a creative outlet into a SMART goal:

SPECIFIC: Start a political blog and add to it every day.

MEASURABLE: I will look back on Sunday evenings and count the number of times I wrote that week.

ACHIEVABLE: This is something I have time for because I can write as much or as little as I want.

RELEVANT: I work in IT for the government and really want a place to express my political opinions. Plus I want to practice writing consistently so I can think about writing a book.

TIME-BOUND: I will check in with my progress in thirty days and reassess from there.

PUT YOURSELF UNDER CONTRACT

✦ ✦ ✦

Quality is never an accident; it is always the result of high intention, sincere effort, intelligent direction and skillful execution.

—WILLIAM A. FOSTER

My phone rang the other evening. It was Dave, a young man with chronic fatigue syndrome who'd read all of my books and was interested in exploring working together. He'd had a number of coaches and therapists. "How do you work?" he asked right off the bat. "Well, you create a contract for what you want to change in your life in three months and then we work together to bring that into being," I explained. "No one's ever asked me to do that," he replied, incredulous. "Maybe that's why you haven't gotten the results you want," I responded. "It's my experience that a contract keeps your desired result front and center and increases your likelihood of success."

Dave was silent on the other end. He'd been used to open-ended therapy that focused primarily on his talking about his problems. I was challenging him to discover what change he was willing to commit to so that I could help him make it happen. "Let me think about it," he finally said.

You're farther along than Dave. You've already discovered your formula for success and created a SMART goal. Now it's time to put it all together by making a contract with yourself that also includes the strategies you will employ to meet your goal. Why put it in writing? Because there's been a lot of research that making a written contract for change really helps people to stick to it. It has been shown to help children study more, keep potential suicides from killing themselves, help people exercise consistently, and keep unemployed folks motivated in job searches. Start with something *really* small and a time frame that's short if that will be motivating. (Remember *kaisen?*) When the contract is up, make another, incorporating what you've learned from this one. Or pick a really big thing if you believe that will be more effective.

When you create your contract, I strongly suggest having a witness sign as well, just as with other kinds of contracts. This is important because it helps signal to yourself the seriousness with which you undertake this change and increases the likelihood you'll follow through. As a friend said, "To save face with those I told, I had to follow through."

Make sure you refer back to your formula for success and include the strategies you will employ to meet your goal. These are the actions you are going to take to get the results you desire. In the exercise contract below, the strategies are dancing, jogging, biking.

Remember the guy who wanted to create a blog in the previous chapter? He and I studied his previous successes and came up with strategies that he included in his contract: get up fifteen minutes early and write in the morning; look at who's coming to the site to get encouragement to keep on. When the month is up, he can modify these strategies depending on the results he's getting. I also encouraged him to reward himself with a mental "good job" as he went out the door each morning he did it well. The more we reward the behavior we want, the more it will increase.

A SIMPLE CONTRACT

Here's one from a client of mine:

I, _____, will move every day for at least seven minutes starting [date] and ending [date]. The movement can be dancing, jogging, biking, anything that gets my heart pumping, and I can do it anytime during the day, as long as I do it. Every day that I keep my promise, I will be sure to appreciate myself before I go to bed.

Signed_____

Date_____

Witnessed_____

BECOME A TRACKER

✦　✦　✦

The secret of success is constancy to purpose.

—BENJAMIN DISRAELI

arah's dream was to become a more confident public speaker. She'd recently gotten a job she really wanted that required a lot of standing up and talking in front of groups. When she created her SMART goal, she'd decided to measure her comfort level on a scale of -5 to +5. She'd had several public speaking engagements since the last time we spoke. I was asking her how it was going. "I'm not sure," she replied. "It's still really scary."

"But have you made progress on getting your number up from -5?" I inquired.

"I'm not sure," she confessed. "I don't think so."

Sarah is like so many of us who try to change something. She didn't know whether she'd improved because she hadn't been tracking her progress. Because change happens in small increments, unless you track yourself, you can't see the improvements you may actually be making. This is particularly true in situations when the measurements are internal—feeling more confident or less worried, for instance.

By creating your SMART goal, you've already figured out *what* you're going to measure—pounds, sense of ease in your body, hours of sleep, times you stay calm with your kids. Now you need to decide how often you should measure and a way to track your measurements. This too can be extremely simple. If it's something you've committed to do daily, like taking time to be thankful at the end of the day, all you need is a chart that has the days down one side. Simply put a check mark next to the days you keep your commitment to yourself. If it's a once a week task—let's say cleaning your desk every Friday—you can put a check mark on a calendar so you can keep track. If it's going from a -4 to a +4 when thinking about flying, you need to write down your number every time you get ready for a trip. You can also keep a diary—journal keepers, say researchers, achieve their goals faster than others.

Don't move forward until you figure out a tracking system. Otherwise, you may be discouraged because you don't experience enough progress or underestimate how far you've come. Tracking what you've done keeps you grounded in the actual facts, rather than in fear or hopefulness: I committed to seven days a week and did it four times. I said I would spend one day per weekend on planning my new business and I have done it three out of four weekends.

People who don't track don't do as well as those who do. It's as simple as that. Trackers do better not only because they can measure success, but because they can mine the data they collect to point them in more successful directions.

That's because the truth can set you free—as long as you look at it as information, not as the chance for self-punishment. (More on that in "Keeping Going.") For right now, begin to think like a scientist. Scientists don't beat themselves up for what they discover. They simply observe, track the results, and make fact-based conclusions regarding next actions on the basis of what they discovered. Emulate Thomas Edison, the creator of the first practical lightbulb and many other modern inventions. As I described in *The Power of Patience,* when someone categorized his seven hundred attempts at the lightbulb as failures, he said, "I have not failed seven hundred times. I have not failed once. I have succeeded in proving that those seven hundred ways will not work. When I eliminate all the ways that don't work, I will find the one that will." It took him one thousand tries.

After talking to me, Sarah decided to get more scientific in her approach. Each time she had a public speaking engagement, she wrote down her number the day before and the day of the event. In analyzing the data, she discovered that she experienced greater ease if she prepared her talk several days in advance rather than waiting till the day before. She also learned that giving the speech to a friend the day before also helped.

The experimental approach can work for you too—"Oh, I thought if I tried doing it in the morning it would be easier to do. But I did it only twice this week. What if I shift to the end of the day? Let's see how I do next week." The more objective you can remain, the less you will fall into the slough of perfectionism or despair that traps so many would-be resolvers and habit changers.

WHAT KIND OF SUPPORT DO YOU NEED?

✦   ✦   ✦

Perfect as the wing of a bird may be, it will never enable the bird to fly if unsupported by air.

—IVAN PAVLOV

was on a four-hour bus ride through the English countryside. About every hour, the bus would stop and a new driver would get on. It was a system, I saw, that enabled each driver never to get too far from home base, for he would then drive the bus going back where he came from. Each time the exchange happened, the drivers would share information about the route: "Avoid the M40; it's all backed up. Take the local route around the church and stay straight until you can hook up ten miles ahead." Because each had been where the other was going, they could give one another real-time information. There were no cell phones, no shortwave radios, no pagers, no walkie-talkies. What a profoundly simple support system. I imagined it had been created in stagecoach days and had continued unabated for centuries.

As we go about living the change we want to see in ourselves, we need to take a lesson from the English bus drivers. We need a way to stay close to home base and learn from other journeyers who have gone before us. Receiving support doesn't mean we're weak, stupid, or needy. It just means that the road ahead is unknown because we haven't traveled on it yet. If we're willing to accept support, we can avoid a great number of potholes and traffic jams that we would otherwise encounter.

I was talking recently to a sixty-year-old man who had dreamed of flying all his life and was working to get a pilot's license. Asking for support was something he'd avoided his whole life. So he'd gone it alone in taking the written test, even though he knew it would be hard for him. "I flunked," he admitted, "and that was a major lesson for me. I realized that if I wanted to make my dream come true, I had to ask for help. I went to my wife and asked her to drill me every evening. The second time, I passed with flying colors. Now I'm about to be tested on instrument flying and you better believe she's helping me prepare."

I don't care who you are or what you are trying to learn. When you're learning something new, it's best to have support. Even if it's only support in remembering your intention. Many of us get stuck or give up because we believe we should fly solo and therefore crash and burn. We're taught that not knowing something is a sign of weakness, so we cut ourselves off from one of the crucial components for success: help from the outside.

All of us know that if we want to learn physics, we've got to seek out a book or a person to teach us. We know we can't just sit there and manifest physics knowledge. But when it comes to changing habits in ourselves or making our dreams manifest, we believe we should somehow miraculously know what to do and how to do it by ourselves.

Support comes in all kinds of forms—someone who's been there before you who can help you avoid pitfalls; a partner who will practice with you; a group of people who are all working on the same thing; a friend who you report to; a coach who helps you stay accountable to yourself; a therapist who can help you uncover long-buried feelings; a board of advisors to help you build your construction business.

The question when you are bringing something new into being in yourself is not *Do I need help?* but *What kind of help do I need?* Melanie Griffith recently acknowledged she goes to AA up to three times a day to stay clean and sober. A friend working on being more grateful has a friend she e-mails her list of what she's thankful for at the end of each day; the friend responds with her own list. I have a workout partner. It helps me to get to the gym, knowing she'll be there too. Sometimes I have clients who leave me a daily message on my voice mail, letting me know how they are progressing on becoming more upbeat or organized.

Support can motivate us, teach us, and remind us of what we're trying to accomplish. At any given moment, you may need one or another of these forms of support. One of the best things outside support can do for us is to help us hold ourselves accountable and create deadlines. This is critical when what you want to bring into being is not asked for from the outside. Organizing your house, starting your own business, writing a memoir, losing twenty pounds—these are things you want to do because you want to. No one is demanding it of you. Without someone to be accountable to, it's easy to slip back to the status quo. When you have a writing group that meets on Tuesday and you have to show up with a sketch, you're more likely to write. When your friend is going to show up at the door to go to yoga class with you, you're more likely to go. When you are going to get weighed in at Tops on Friday, you're more likely to stick to your weight-loss plan. Outside support structures help us keep our promises to ourselves. Weight Watchers, for instance, claims that people who use its support group are three times more likely to lose weight than folks on their own.

Of course, support does not have to come only from people. It can also be found in books, music, the Internet, drives in the car, long walks, swimming, inspiring quotes—anything that helps you do what you want in your life. Don't discount legal chemical support too. Our brain chemistry has a lot to do with the actions we do or don't take. If you are seriously depressed or extremely anxious, it's hard to get into motion or sustain forward action. And if you are subject to binge behavior of any sort—sex, eating, drinking, shopping—it could be your dopamine level is out of whack. Dopamine has been shown to inhibit impulsive behavior and improper dopamine function has been associated with addictions of all sorts.

In thinking about the change you want to make, what kind of support do you need right now? One way to begin to answer the question is to ask yourself: when I've accomplished something in the past, who or what helped me do it? Any accomplishment will do. Now think of another. What helped you do that? Think about a third. Is a pattern emerging of the kind of support you need?

Elizabeth's dream was to buy a house. When moving time came, lots of friends offered to help. She was completely overwhelmed as to what kind of help she needed until she remembered that in the past, the best help she ever got was from her friend Mona, "the voice of reason," as Elizabeth calls her. "As usual, in eight minutes, she helped me figure out a plan of attack. Then I went off happily to move."

When I thought about my pattern of support, here's what emerged: I first get support by reading about others who have done what I want to do. Then I start practicing and talking to my friends about what I'm learning. They give me other ideas. The talking also reinforces what I've learned. I then write about it, which helps me ratchet my learning up a notch. When it's something I don't like to do, I do best with a buddy so I can't wiggle out of it.

What works for you?

NO MORE FEAR OF FLYING

"I was a panicked flyer until my sixties," says Annette Madden. "I generally avoided it or would down two glasses of wine before takeoff so I could get on the plane. Then I got interested in researching my family tree and wanted to fly more often. When I found myself vomiting for two days before a flight with anticipatory anxiety, I decided to do something. Toughing it out was making it worse. Listening to friends tell me it was no big deal was useless. Fear of flying courses didn't seem right. Being a person who used therapy in the past, I decided on hypnosis. I put the word out to everyone I knew to get a recommendation for a good hypnotherapist. I did four sessions. Then she made me a tape to listen to before I flew and while I was on the plane. It was like magic—no more fear of flying!"

IT'S GOING TO FEEL AWKWARD AT FIRST

You must break out of your current comfort zone and become comfortable with the unfamiliar and the unknown.

—DENIS WAITLEY

Jon Carroll is a writer for the *San Francisco Chronicle*. I read him every morning. The other day, his column opened this way: "So the new thing this year is that Tracy and I are taking waltz lessons at Big Al's Brainlock Ballroom where the concepts of 'left' and 'right' turn out to be a lot more subtle than I had originally thought. Also: What is this 'on the beat' they speak of? It is, however, wonderful fun, although not perhaps for anyone watching."

Now you know why I love him—he's very funny. Smart too. Because whether he knows it consciously or not, he knows that when you first begin to do something new or different, *you are not very good at it.*

This may seem obvious, but you can't believe how often it gets in our way. We feel awkward—tongue-tied, all thumbs, as if we've got two left feet—and we take it as a sign to go back to the tried and true. Even if the tried and true is a prison cell, we long for the comfort of the familiar. As a friend says, "Be it ever so toxic, there's no place like home."

But to learn anything, we have to leave the comfort of the known for the awkwardness of the untried. And we must accept our ineptness as the price of beginning, trusting that, like adolescents, we'll grow out of that awkward stage and blossom into mastery if we just hang in there.

I'll never forget the first time that I had to stand up in front of a corporate group as a consultant and do a presentation. Talk about a stretch! It was a Fortune 50 company paying a lot of money for leadership development and I had just switched that week from being a book editor for twenty-five years. I guess I did okay—I was asked back. But someone in the room who saw me present six months later remarked that she couldn't believe how much better I'd gotten. So obviously my awkwardness was apparent on the outside too. But I would not have the career I do today if I hadn't been willing to endure the discomfort that comes with stretching beyond my previous experience.

You absolutely can't change anything if you stay in the familiar. That's the place where you get what you've always gotten. That's what makes it comfortable—the habit of it, the "I do this all the time." Any time you break out of that place, it's going to feel weird: What do you do with your hands if you're not smoking? What else can you do with your time besides go to the mall on Saturdays and spend money you don't have? No, all hell won't break loose if you sit down and work on your writing before checking your e-mails; it just feels that way. And yes, you may have trouble knowing left from right when you first begin to waltz.

Someone once told me that people who change can tolerate anxiety better than those who stay stuck. I take that to mean that they are able to stand being awkward. That awkward feeling is actually a good thing—it's a sign you're learning. We at Professional Thinking Partners teach our clients that there are three zones of existence: comfort, stretch, and stress. Stretch is where change occurs. It's where you feel awkward, but not so stressed out that learning is impossible. Imagine you decide to learn to ski. The comfort zone would be sitting at home. The stretch zone might be the bunny slope. And the stress zone would be a black diamond run.

These zones are moving targets. If you practice on the bunny slope, it then becomes your comfort zone. Eventually the black diamond run becomes your stretch zone. So remember, if what you're doing doesn't feel at least somewhat weird to you, you haven't yet gone far enough out of your comfort zone for change to happen.

Getting into the stretch zone is good for you in general, by the way. It helps keep your brain healthy. It turns out that unless we continue to learn new things, which challenges our brains to create new pathways, they literally begin to atrophy, which may result in dementia, Alzheimer's, and other brain diseases. Continuously stretching ourselves will even help us lose weight, according to one study. Researchers who asked folks to do something different every day—listen to a new radio station, for instance—found that they lost and kept off weight. No one is sure why, but scientists speculate that getting out of routines makes us more aware in general.

The implication of all of this is that we should welcome awkwardness when we're creating a new habit; it's the sign our brain is creating a pathway that will eventually make us proficient. When I help beginning writers, I always tell them, spew and then review. Just get it out, no matter how badly. You can clean it up later. Those who were willing to do that finished their books; the ones who couldn't are still stuck.

But since we live in a culture that reveres comfort, it can be very challenging to feel awkward or do something badly. So I encourage my clients to announce their beginner status when appropriate to remind themselves and others that they may not do things "perfectly": "I'm new at this apologizing stuff so bear with me", "I'm just beginning to articulate my vision for my company so I need you to listen without criticizing"; "I'm just learning how to have fun without drinking. Can you help me?"

Moving into the stretch zone takes courage. That's one of the reasons why changing habits or following your dream is character building. It requires that you take a risk—the risk of looking foolish, the risk of falling flat on your face. But as Stephen Covey reminds us, "The greatest risk is of riskless living." Because we can never get to where we want to go from the comfort zone. So get out on that dance floor and give it your best shot. It will get easier. I promise.

KEEPING A JOURNAL:
"AT FIRST I DIDN'T HAVE MUCH TO SAY"

"It started when I went back to college," professional photographer and speaker Mark Sincevich explains. "I had a lot of aspirations, but I wasn't very successful keeping them in the same place. I took a class on journal writing. The best advice the instructor said was to always keep your journal with you. At first I didn't have much to say. I just stared at it. Then I started using it as a sort of scrapbook pasting in train tickets, photographs, and even flowers. I began commenting on the things I put there. I kept at it because I felt that I was digging at the surface of tremendous power. After a few months of commenting and always carrying it with me, I formed a habit. I realized I was tapping into my inner voice, that river of imaginable ideas. It's now sixteen years later and I have filled over forty journals. I use it to relax when I am stressed. It allows me to put all of my thoughts in one place and to sort out exactly what I want to say. I use it to do my draft business and marketing plan and to plan my budgets, both personal and professional. I have various reminders and lists in my journal. It helps me make sure that I am headed in the right direction in my life!"

YES, YOU CAN FIND THE TIME

✦   ✦   ✦

Time is a created thing. To say "I don't have time" is to say, "I don't want to."

—LAO TZU

All of the people I work with feel time starved. They have too many tasks to accomplish in a day, a week, a month, or a year. Some come to me precisely because they want help in focusing, in figuring out what to pay attention to and what to let go of. Others are trying to get healthy or have a better family life but "have no time." They deal with the immense workload by working more. Most are drastically sleep deprived and, as a consequence, are impaired in their capacity to think rationally or take things in stride. Not one thinks he or she has any options.

Renee was one such client. The head of a hundred people involved in a variety of complex projects, she would arrive home from the office around 8, fix dinner for herself and her husband, then answer e-mails from ten o'clock to midnight or 1 A.M., sleep for four or five hours and get to the office by 7 to begin it all again. Every day. She knew she needed time for sleep and exercise but it felt impossible.

I asked her what would happen if she left her computer at the office in the evenings. She was sure that disaster would strike. I challenged her to try it for a week. The next time we spoke she exclaimed, "It's amazing. If I answer e-mails at night, a slew of responses await me in the morning. If I don't answer until the morning, the responses come a bit later. I'm not slowing the volume down by staying up all night. Nor am I speeding up the projects significantly. The only effect taking a few hours to myself is having is on me—positively."

What Renee discovered, to her happy amazement, was that she could take back daily time for herself without the sky falling. And that's no small thing. So many of us, particularly women, believe not only that we are totally indispensable (or should be), but that we must sacrifice anything and everything we might need to keep the world turning. And we fool ourselves into believing we have no choice in the matter.

The truth is, of course, that every day, every single one of us who is not imprisoned or enslaved chooses where and how to focus our time. Those around us—bosses, family members, friends—may gladly take advantage of our willingness to choose everyone and everything but ourselves. But we shouldn't fool ourselves that it's not our choice.

Renee got another strong lesson in this one day when she was complaining about a colleague. "He never stays late and he's considered the golden boy. How does he keep up with all the demands?" "Ask him," I suggested. When she did, he told her, "I ignore everything I don't consider important." "I could never do that," said Renee. "If I don't respond to everyone, I'll feel bad."

Each of us has the choice as to how we spend our time. But it's really easy to tell ourselves it's not our choice, especially when it involves some new habit or dream that takes energy to bring into being.

I know I can easily fall into the "no time" trap when it comes to exercising. But as Lao-Tzu reminds us, what I'm really saying to myself is I don't want to work out. And so I challenge myself to quit making excuses and get back out to the gym. If that means my family will not have a fancy homemade dinner or that my to-do list gets even longer, that's the price I'll have to pay. To-do lists are endless anyway.

This is not to say finding the time is easy. It may require sacrifice. Organizing your closets instead of watching TV. Using vacation time to take a course rather than to relax. Not visiting your aging mother as much as you "should." In some senses, the trade-offs we make reveal what we really care about. I remember once reading about Sylvia Plath. She was a young divorcee with two small children when she wrote some of her best poetry—at 4 or 5 A.M., before the kids woke. That's how much she wanted it.

Time is one of our most precious resources. Even if you can carve out only fifteen minutes a day to devote to your new habit, that's ninety-one hours over the course of a year. What time choices do you need to make so you can have what you really want?

EXERCISING: "I BEGAN STEALING BACK THE TIME"

"I'm in a job where eighty-hour weeks are not unusual," says Mark. "Yet I make sure that I get an hour of exercise every day. When I tried to make myself schedule it in, it didn't work. But then someone asked me to think of an occasion when in the midst of a busy work life I'd taken time for what mattered to me. Instantly the birth of my son came to mind. Despite flying around the country, I was there at his birth and for almost every dinnertime for the following eight years. I could do it because I vowed that the company was not going to take my family time. When I thought about this in connection with exercising, I realized that *I* was part of my family too and if I didn't take care of myself, I was cheating them. I didn't have to get to the office at 6 A.M.—that hour didn't belong to my company, it belonged to me. I'd been choosing to give it to them. I began stealing back the time for myself by working out daily at 6. I went from being thirty-five pounds heavier and an occasional gym member to being in the best shape of my life at age forty-one.

WHEN YOU DON'T KNOW WHAT TO DO,
CHANNEL SOMEONE WHO DOES

✦　✦　✦

Most people live, whether physically, intellectually or morally, in a very restricted circle of their potential being. They make use of a very small portion of their possible consciousness, and of their soul's resources in general, much like a man who, out of his whole bodily organism, should get into a habit of using and moving only his little finger.

—WILLIAM JAMES

Tricia came to me to work on getting more organized. Nothing she'd ever done so far worked—or at least not for long. Looking at her formula for success in other realms wasn't helping. I was getting desperate. "Who's the most organized person you know?" I asked. "My friend Lucy," she replied. "Okay," I said, "what would Lucy do right now?" "Well, she'd unpack her suitcase before checking her e-mail." "How about if you try that?" And off Tricia went, having been instructed to keep asking what would Lucy do and doing it.

I love this little "trick." It's a way of getting to an answer for yourself when you are stuck. For of course you are the one coming up with the answer. Lucy isn't there. For all you know she may not unpack her suitcase for days. But somehow thinking through someone else's eyes gives us access to inner resources we otherwise couldn't discover. When Tricia thinks habitually, she comes in the door, sees the mess, and feels overwhelmed yet again. When she thinks like Lucy, she gets out of her own way and a solution pops up.

What this really means, of course, is that Tricia actually does know somewhere in her mind how to get and stay organized. But habit prevents her from enacting what she knows. By pretending to be someone else, she circumvents her habit.

You can do this for anything. An incredibly poised friend in her mid-thirties told me she grew up very shy and had a difficult time in social settings until she saw a Katharine Hepburn movie in her college years and realized she could present herself like Hepburn. "I loved how forthright she was, without trying to be funny or put on airs. To this day, when I speak or interact, I try to channel the three qualities I ascribe to her: courageous, honest, and generous." Want to be happier? Think of the happiest person you know. Then do what he would do. Want to be calm? Think of the calmest person you can think of and imagine how she'd respond.

In *The Art of Changing*, Susan Peabody talks about using her daughter Kathy this way. "When we're together I take cues from her. If we're at the supermarket and people are annoying, she stays calm. Every time I start to get upset, I just look at her and think, if she can stay polite, so can I. When we're apart, I frequently ask myself, 'What would Kathy do in this situation?' Then I do it."

There's a variation on this that also works. Think of someone you care deeply about—your sibling, a dear friend, your spouse. Imagine they've come to you for advice on the exact problem you are having. What would you tell them to do? Whenever I challenge someone to do this, they always come up with all kinds of great suggestions. After they've finished, I ask a question: "Are you willing to take your own advice?" Usually there is dead silence on the other end of the line as the person absorbs what's just happened. Most bravely go off to give it a try and usually report greater success than with any idea I could have come up with.

The reason these techniques work is because, as motivational writer Taro Gold says, "everything you need to break unhealthy cycles of behavior is within you." Yes, support from others can be invaluable. Yes, watching others may lead you to try something you've never thought about before. But most often, somewhere deep inside of you, you already have the answer you are seeking. You've just got to do the hard work of remembering and applying it today. And when it comes to that, it sometimes helps to channel someone else.

OOPS, I FORGOT

✦　✦　✦

Habits are cobwebs at first; cables at last.

—CHINESE PROVERB

recently went on a twelve-day business trip to Europe with two colleagues. One said to me as we got on the plane, "I'm watching my weight. Will you help me eat right by reminding me to eat salads and chicken?" One night we'd been working late and were sitting around waiting to go out to dinner with others. My dieting friend arrived with several bags of chips for the group. As he tore into one, I privately reminded him of his request. "I completely forgot," he replied. "Thanks for reminding me."

Scientists tell us that the amount of time between impulse and action is half a second. *Half a second.* We really don't give it any thought. An impulse arises and in a blink we're doing what we've always done because whatever pathway we've already created operates at warp speed. We've got our hand in the cookie jar, the liquor to our lips, the inexcusable insult hurled at our spouse. So to learn something new, we've absolutely got to increase our awareness so we have a choice between impulse and action.

Awareness equals the potential for freedom from our habituated mind. A recent study showed that thinking about what you ate at lunch before eating an afternoon snack resulted in an average fourteen-pound weight loss. That's how powerful simple awareness is. Paul Ekman, former head of the Human Interaction Lab at the University of California at San Francisco, studied emotions for fifty years. In a recent article in *Shambala Sun,* he said, "When I completed my training forty-five years ago, my supervisor said, "If you can increase the gap between impulse and action, you will benefit your patient."

Such awareness is the best friend we can have in creating a new habit. It's like the pause button on the TV. With awareness, the impulse arises and we get to decide what course of action we're going to take. What would be the outcome of yelling at my child? Am I going to be happy later if I drink this now? Will it help me to be more organized if I just throw this on the floor of my closet?

This pause doesn't even take very long. Someone once told me that awareness also only takes a half second. I believe that's because if you are clear on what you want and why, you don't actually go through the process of asking yourself questions such as the ones in the paragraph above. It's more of a semiautomatic "Oh, yeah, I don't want to do this anymore." Or "Remember, I've decided to do this."

So how are you going to remember to press the pause button? Whenever I ask my clients this, there's dead silence. Most of us haven't been taught awareness strategies. But in the beginning, like my dieting friend, you absolutely need some kind of reminder from the outside. Not because you're weak or bad but because your habit cables are so strong. You forget and then you beat yourself up for forgetting.

Avoid the shame cycle by putting awareness jogs into place. Stress and fitness expert Dr. Pamela Peeke suggests posting stickies on the fridge and food or liquor bottles that say, "The answer is not here." I tell clients who want to learn to be more grateful to post a note on their steering wheel, "What am I thankful for right now?" Every time they see the sign, they have to answer the question. Put a picture on your desk of the way you want it to look. Ask a friend to e-mail you every day with a note saying, "What have you done to advance your business idea to-day?" I once helped a friend buy a ring that was her reminder to treat her mother with patience. While talking to her face to face or on the phone, she'd fiddle with the ring to remember her intention.

You can also increase awareness by temptation-proofing your environment. Cut up your credit cards or put them in the freezer so that the next time you go to whip them out, they're not there. Then you'll remember you don't want to spend. Get rid of your chips, cookies, and ice cream. Then when you find yourself scrounging in the cupboards, you'll remember you've chosen not to indulge in such items.

If you are giving up something addictive, you may need to avoid the places and people associated with indulging. That's because the body develops a physical response to the environments it was in when you indulged. Psychologists call it conditioned cravings—the surroundings or time of day or familiar faces have been so connected to the substance that your body begins to create intense cravings that are hard to resist.

Find something else to do at five o'clock if that was your daily cocktail hour. Avoid parties for a while. If you have to have candy at the movies and are losing weight, don't go to the movies. If you're trying to control your temper with your spouse and always fight at Home Depot, avoid Home Depot for a while. When my husband first stopped smoking pot, he asked his friends not to indulge around him. That helped a lot, he says. Otherwise his old habit would have just taken over.

Asking others to be your awareness partners can be tricky. The last thing you need is to have someone nag at you. "You promised me you'd never smoke again!" I used to cry hysterically at my now-ex every time I caught him with a cigarette. It was highly ineffective. He started doing it behind my back; I was always suspicious. That is one of the potential pitfalls of enlisting help—you could start to sneak around.

If human reminders cause too much tension, rely on more impersonal technologies—notes, scheduling awareness strategies in your day planner, screen savers, e-mails you set up to be sent to you automatically. You may find that you have to keep inventing new awareness jogs as your brain gets used to the old ones and they become part of the background. If you no longer notice the sign on the computer saying "remember to breathe before picking up phone," it's time to put it somewhere else. Or come up with a new reminder. You can set your computer to buzz every hour to remind you to take three breaths.

If you want to increase the possibility of success, be sure to put such reminders in place. I promise that you won't need them forever—just long enough for the new habit to become the new default. Then the habit cable will be one you'll rely on, not be imprisoned by.

GETTING REMINDERS THAT TRULY HELP

Here are a few tips to avoid destructive dynamics when asking others to help you remember what you've resolved:

1. You must be the one who makes the request for awareness support.

2. Pick someone without a vested interest—It was not the wife of the dieter who asked for a reminder. He may have bristled at her more than at me.

3. You must be explicit about what kind of reminder you would like. It's probably not a lecture, just something simple like "Did you write your ten pages today?" Or it could be a code between the two of you, like the words "yellow submarine," to help keep you from mindlessly eating the donut in front of you.

4. The other person must deliver the reminder and then back off—follow-through is up to you.

MAKE BACKUP PLANS, NOT EXCUSES

✦ ✦ ✦

Ninety-nine percent of the failures come from people who have the habit of making excuses.

—GEORGE WASHINGTON CARVER

M ost of my clients are serious about changing. They've put their money where their mouth is to work with me, which is a sign of serious commitment and intention. And, despite inevitable setbacks along the way, for the most part they do change. Maybe not as much or as fast as they would prefer. But they do.

Occasionally, however, I happen upon folks who don't seem to ever create forward momentum. They commit to an action when we speak and then they show up next time with all the reasons why they haven't done it. The excuses tend to fall into two categories: "It's all my fault" (I'm lazy, disorganized, stupid, undisciplined) or "The circumstances are beyond my control" (business meetings, kid got sick, dog peed on the project). The first group is expert at negative self-analysis. The second group is great at blaming everything and everyone else.

Life is good at throwing us curveballs that get in our way, particularly when it comes to changing a habit or doing something different. Because more energy is required to change than to stay the same, it's easier to get thrown off a new course. That's why I love the recommendation of Pamela Peeke in *Fight Fat After Forty*: create contingency plans up front. Because any number of curveballs may knock you down, she says, not only should you have a backup plan, but have backups to your backups. That way you won't lose momentum. You won't have to stop because you've already figured out what you're going to do. And you won't give up in despair because you've already got another way forward. Here's how management expert Lester R. Bittel puts it: "Good plans shape good decisions. That's why good planning helps to make elusive dreams come true."

I had just finished reading Dr. Peeke's advice one fine summer day when I got the chance to practice. I put the book down and drove to the gym, only to discover it was closed due to a family emergency. Okay, I thought to myself, I need Plan B. I'll go home and swim in my pool. At that very moment it turned cold and started raining, which never happens in the summer in Walnut Creek, California. By now I was laughing. Okay, universe, I get the message. Putting on my raincoat, I went to Plan C—walking as fast as I could for thirty minutes.

It was an important lesson for me, and not just about keeping my own commitment to fitness. I realized that I had not been serving my excuse-making clients very well. I had not helped them create contingency plans, which had led some of them to blame themselves and others to blame everything else. I began asking at the end of our sessions, "What's Plan B? If you can't do this in the way we've just discussed, what's your backup?" It was extremely helpful to them to create alternate scenarios; their rate of success skyrocketed.

Like my clients, rather than getting bogged down after the fact in excuses, which only makes you feel bad and gets in the way of success, how about planning for things going wrong? You will have business meetings that will mess with your commitment to get enough sleep. You will be pressed for time and have to feed the kids in a hurry despite your "no more junk food" resolution. The job you thought you had in the bag may indeed fall through.

What are your contingency plans? What are you going to do about your commitment to writing in your journal daily when your mother comes to town? What are Plans A, B, and C now that you've given up drinking and you've just been invited to a bar for a business meeting? How are you going to meet that special someone if you try eharmony.com with no success?

Make contingency plans and you'll find you don't need excuses. Miraculously, you won't be lazy or undisciplined. And you'll know just what to do when the dog pees on the report.

HOW COMMITTED ARE YOU?

"Out of ten," writes Canadian coach Michael Bungay Stanier, "how would you score your current commitment? Now you've done that, realize that this is a trick question. There is no 'halfway' on commitment. You either are, or are not ... ask yourself this question: if people were watching you, how would they know that you were committed?" In other words, would they see actions that support your commitment?

USE YOUR IMAGINATION TO
MAKE IT EASIER

✦　✦　✦

If you want to reach a goal, you must "see the reaching" in your own mind before you actually arrive at your goal.

—ZIG ZIGLAR

Years ago, there was a famous study done on champion skiers training for the Olympics. One group did their normal training on the slopes. The other didn't ski at all. Rather, they vividly imagined themselves making every run correctly. When it came to game time, the imaginers skied better than the others. The results were so astounding that since then, imagining a peak performance is one of the techniques high-performance athletes use regularly.

How does it work? It turns out that if the process is vivid enough the brain does not differentiate between imagining doing something and actually doing it. Either way our neurons are firing that particular sequence, making it easier to do it again. There's an upside and a downside to this. The downside is that when we imagine scary possibilities and gloomy outcomes, we train our brains to get that result. The upside is that we can use this "trick" to make changing a habit or learning something new easier.

This understanding is what spawned a whole industry of affirmations and visualizations. But often these don't work for two reasons. First, because each of these is incomplete. We actually need to imagine success in the three ways in which we experience the world—seeing, hearing, and feeling—in order for the brain to make new pathways. We have to see, hear, and feel ourselves in the situation as if it were actually happening. Merely saying "I will be thin" or just picturing yourself in a bikini won't work.

Second, in order for this to be effective, you need to *vividly* imagine yourself in the situation. In Technicolor, as it were. If you're quitting smoking, for instance, you better believe that your wanting to smoke is a vivid imagining. Trying to write a new program in your brain, as it were, requires an *even more* vivid envisioning. Otherwise you are just wasting your breath chanting "I will be smoke free."

Here's an example. Louise came to me because she wanted help finishing her novel. One of the first things I had her do was to envision the book already done and sitting on her shelf, then take a blank book and create the title and cover she saw. She now sets it beside her computer as a reminder of where she's heading. Then we worked on her seeing, hearing, and feeling herself typing on the computer, writing the last page, sending it off to an agent, having it accepted by a publisher, and opening the box of books on publication day. She imagined it all down to the smell of the cardboard box.

And it did make it easier for her to do. She'd been trying to finish for four years. After our work, she was done in six months. Now that she's learned the process, she can use that same "making the future real" for anything else—the new house she wants to live in, the relationship she wants to have.

So can you. Just remember to explicitly experience what you want in all sensory modes and make it absolutely as real as possible. Your brain will reward you by firing in the exact sequence you'll need when you actually do it. When it comes to successful performance, mental rehearsal can be as good as actually doing it—as long as you make it real to yourself.

A BETTER WORK RELATIONSHIP: "I ENVISION MY BOSS AS A PEER"

"A friend told me of her technique for improving her love life—she visualizes the kind of outgoing woman she wants to be and then acts her way into it," explains Carol. "That gave me the idea to try something similar with my boss, whom I've been intimidated by for several years. Before we have a meeting, I see her and me as peers in age and experience. I feel my confidence and calm. Then I say to myself, 'I have something useful to say and so does she.' It has really helped me to speak my mind more readily and effectively. And we're getting better business results."

DON'T DESPAIR: UNDERSTAND THE THREE STAGES OF LEARNING

✦   ✦   ✦

The closer you get to the lighthouse, the darker it gets.

—JAPANESE PROVERB

ndrea was distraught. "I promised to enjoy my life more this year. But this week, all I've done is stress out over the report I have due tomorrow and run around so fast that I never even once noticed the flowers in my garden or sat quietly for ten minutes as I promised myself I would do."

"Actually," I replied, "I'm happy to report that you're making progress."

"You've got to be kidding," she responded. "I totally screwed up!"

"Perhaps, but you noticed you blew it. Congratulations."

What Andrea didn't know—and chances are you don't either—is that learning happens in three phases. The first is called POST HOC, meaning after the fact you recognize that you wanted to do it differently. This is the "I told myself last week I would remember to be patient with my mother" stage, the "I just remembered I was going to check for jobs on Monster.com yesterday" stage. Believe it or not, learning is happening because before this you're not aware enough to know what's going on at all.

The second is **AD HOC**, meaning that while it's happening you're aware you want to do it differently. That's where another client, Sandy, is in her anger management learning curve: "As I was about to yell at my husband, I thought to myself, walk away, walk away. Then I thought screw it, and let him have it right between the eyes." This is the "I shouldn't buy this cookie (wine, pair of $200 pants) but I'm going to anyway" stage, the "I should turn off this computer and spend more time with my family but I'm still sitting here" stage.

The third is **PRE HOC**, which means you've learned it so well that you've got it in place before anything happens. "You'll be proud of me," reported Lucy, who'd been learning about becoming more organized. "I vowed to keep my house clean through the holidays and I did it, no problem!" This is when you're doing exactly what it is you want to on a regular basis, with more successes than mistakes.

Here's the dirty little secret—you've got to pass through stages one and two to get to three. It's just how learning happens. And it can feel like you're making no progress at all because by definition you are exquisitely aware of how and when you're blowing it. And unless you understand this and learn what to do about it, you can stay stuck in stage one or two forever.

This is crucial to understand. If I could leave you with only one tip for changing anything in your life, it would be this: *recognizing you've blown it is progress!* That's why I love the quote about the lighthouse that opens this chapter, why "it's always darkest before the dawn."

There's always a phase in creating forward motion when all you notice is how hard it is and how little you've moved.

Now comes the delicate part. Whether you move forward has everything to do with how you treat yourself once you notice you've blown it. The trick is to learn from the experience without judging yourself negatively so you don't get discouraged and give up in defeat. (That's why growth orientation, from "Preparing to Change," is so important.)

Here's what I teach my clients to say to themselves: Great. I'm learning. Otherwise I wouldn't even notice I've screwed up. What can I take from this experience for next time? When Andrea asked herself that question, she realized that she hadn't created any reminders for herself to sit quietly or take a stroll through her garden. She posted a big note on both sides of her front door so she could see it coming and going. Every time she noticed it, she was to do one or the other action right then. "I'm encouraged," she said the next time we met. "I'm doing a bit better. Now when I get worked up into a frenzy, I recognize it while it's happening."

We can move through the stages of learning something new. But only if we're willing to treat ourselves encouragingly in the early parts so that we keep our spirits up, remind our brains that we are making progress, and mine our experiences for tomorrow's efforts.

SHOW UP, WITH GRIT

✦   ✦   ✦

Eighty percent of success is showing up.

—WOODY ALLEN

I once had a friend who was a smoker. He'd stopped many times over the years. But always—a week, a month, or a year later—he started again. Once, when he was in a nonsmoking phase, I asked how it was going. "Oh, it's not hard, I've done it a million times," he said.

I knew then that this time wasn't going to work either. It *is* hard, bloody hard. And not acknowledging that to himself was part of what kept him falling back. Until he recognized how hard it was for him to stick to his goal, he never would put in place the strategies he needed to get through the hard times. I remember once, about a year after my husband stopped smoking pot, he turned to me and said, "You know, I'm glad it's illegal. Because if I could buy dope at the corner store, I'm not sure I could stay straight." He admitted to himself that it was difficult and, ironically, the admission set him free. It allowed him to show up in a dedicated way and accept the challenge.

Changing long-standing habits and ways of being *can* be extremely hard. Particularly, of course, when it involves substances that are physically addicting, like alcohol and drugs, including nicotine. Or compulsive eating or anorexia. But because of the way our brains are structured—to run the programs they already run—even changing mental habits can be quite a feat. I've recently been working with a self-described angry worrywart in her mid-twenties who wants to be more positive, grateful, and patient. "I can't believe how hard it is!" she has exclaimed on more than one occasion. I always point out that she's smart to learn now; imagine how grooved in the negative habits would be when she's fifty-three like me.

The fact that it's hard is why, if you really want to change something or bring something into being, you've got to make the commitment to show up to accept the change as the challenge it is. I recently read a piece about Ivana Chubbuck, the acting coach for Brad Pitt, Halle Berry, and Charlize Theron. She said about her successful students: "The students who have made it all had an incredible work ethic. And tremendous tenacity of spirit. Brad worked three jobs and lived with five people to afford classes." What you want to do may require equivalent determination and effort. This is no piece of cake, no walk in the park, no bed of roses. If it were, you wouldn't need a book to help you. You would have already done it.

Showing up is a mental, emotional, and spiritual act that expresses commitment. You acknowledge that this is serious business and that you are up to the challenge. My client Coni is the best personification of this that I know. A single mother of three boys, one of whom is autistic, she has a life full of financial, relational, and circumstantial challenges. I've had the privilege of watching her blossom in many ways over the past four years. Once she's clear that a change must be made, no matter how difficult—in her living situation, her relationship with others, or herself—and we've talked through what she needs to do, she always says four magic words: "I can do that." And then she does. She's built a successful business that way, ended unhealthy relationships, learned to exercise and eat right. That's showing up—for herself, her sons, her life.

When we show up, we exhibit grit. Grit is the determination to succeed, which, according to recent studies at the University of Pennsylvania, may be as important as ability. Researchers there found that folks with grit are more likely to achieve success in school, work, and other undertakings because, scientists speculate, their passion and commitment help them endure the inevitable setbacks that occur in any long-term project.

I don't think grit is something you have or don't. It's a quality you create when you make the choice to show up for what you really want for yourself, no matter how difficult.

SPEAKING UP: "WALK THROUGH THE FEAR"

"I've never been good about saying what I really want," said Maria. "Partly it's because I often don't know what I want. But often it's because I hate to rock the boat. So I just go along with the other person.

This year I resolved to finally speak my emotional truth, particularly to the guy I've been dating for two years. First I began journaling a lot to get clear on what my truth was. Then, before he and I would meet, I'd give myself a pep talk: you can say what's true for you, I'd remind myself. When we got together, I'd challenge myself by thinking, We need to have this conversation. Stop editing. Tell him your truth. At first I had to overcome a great deal of fear. Of what I'm not completely sure. But it gets easier each time and I get a little smoother at it. I see I can survive even when saying something he totally disagrees with. A bonus is that I find it easier to speak up to others as well. The trick was to first get clear about what I want and then to challenge myself to walk through the fear."

DO A POSTGAME REVIEW

✦ ✦ ✦

Even if you are on the right track, you'll get run over if you just sit there.

—WILL ROGERS

lenn, an extremely ambitious, high-powered executive, came to work with me. He was the kind of guy who measures his worth in hours spent at the office. His boss had suggested our partnership because he wasn't totally pleased with his performance. In particular, Glenn wasn't good at listening. He tended just to push his own agenda.

Glenn and I spoke of the importance of his learning to ask questions. His homework was to notice for two weeks how many questions he asked in meetings versus how many statements he made. When we next met, I asked him how he'd done. "I've been so busy I haven't had time to think about it," he confessed. "I think I'm doing better but I'm not sure."

I explained to him that reflection after an event accelerates learning. He looked at me as if I'd just flown in from Mars. I don't think he'd ever reflected on himself or his behavior in his entire life. Then I had a moment of inspiration. I knew he loved football and so I said, "You know how after the game, the coach and players get together and do an analysis of how they did so they can do even better next week? That's what I'm talking about. A postgame review."

"Oh," he said, the lightbulb going on. Suddenly he was fully engaged. We proceeded to devise a system where, rather than go directly to thinking about what he had to do next, which was his habit, he would do a postgame review as he was walking or driving away from every meeting.

What Glenn discovered is what you will too, if you practice doing a postgame review. It keeps what we're trying to learn front and center. Tracking his number of questions after a meeting made it easier for him to remember to ask questions at the next meeting. Pretty soon, he could do it automatically. He—and his boss—were pleased.

Reflection also accelerates learning because it gives us a chance to evaluate how we're doing and course correct. What worked? How could I do it even better next time? Those are the two best reflection questions I know because they lead your mind to reinforce success—do more of this—and consider improvement, without falling into shame or guilt. I once worked with a leadership group for nine months, helping them become a high-performance team. Each week they got better and better at thinking together simply by asking these two questions at the end of their meetings.

How and when will you reflect on your performance? You've already created your SMART goal—for instance, to spend two hours per week doing just what you want for yourself. So perhaps you decide that you'll reflect each Monday morning as you drive to work. What worked?

"Well, I didn't get two hours, but I did get a whole hour to read some of the novel that's been sitting by my bedside on Saturday afternoon when Ted took the kids to soccer." What could be improved upon? "Oh, I see it's not easy to get the two hours in a row. This week, I'm going to aim for one hour on the weekend and one hour on Tuesday when the kids go to bed." Then next Monday, you repeat the two questions, readjusting and restrategizing until you find the formula that works.

I can't encourage you enough to add this postgame review to your repertoire. It's one of the best ways to achieve the greatest success.

AA IS ON TO SOMETHING—
ONE DAY AT A TIME

✦ ✦ ✦

We do this one day at a time in a row.

—CRAIG (posted on a recovery website)

was talking to a friend who recently came to understand that she had
to stop drinking. "My mind is a very funny thing," Leslie proclaimed.
"If I think to myself I can never drink again, all I want to do is drink.
And I think all kinds of unhelpful things. My recent favorite is 'But this
means I can't drink champagne at my daughter's wedding.' How ridicu-
lous can I be? She's six, with no marriage candidates in sight!"

AA and other twelve-step programs are full of wisdom about change.
One of my favorites is "one day at a time." You don't have to stop drinking forever—you just have to get through today without drinking. Then
when tomorrow comes, you do it again. That's a very intelligent strategy
because as soon as you think "never" or "forever," your mind immediately throws up all kinds of resistance. Forever is just too darn long.
Never is just too hard. But today? Anyone can do today.

You don't have to be an addict for this to be useful. I know if I tell myself I have to exercise every day for the rest of my life, my first response is to want to lie down and never get up. But when I say, you've got to exercise today, then it becomes possible.

I used to think the reason for this is that we are all weak, screwed-up human beings. But then I read *Driven by Wellth* by Julie Maloney and Renee Moorefield. In it, I came across an alternative explanation that I've found extremely useful. All living systems, including humans, they explain, are hardwired to adapt *and* hardwired to keep their integrity by remaining the same. Without the capacity to adapt, we wouldn't evolve—as individuals or species. But without the capacity to resist change, we'd all lose our individuality and morph into whatever we came across. Psychologist Dominique De Backer explains it this way in a recent O magazine article: "the brain will accept new information only if it doesn't jeopardize or harm the coherence the brain is trying to maintain."

When we try to make changes that are too aggressive, our system tries to maintain the status quo by swinging in the opposite direction. This is one of the reasons, for instance, why strict diets don't work. Telling yourself never to let chocolate pass your lips brings on an instantaneous intense desire for ten pounds of chocolate as your system struggles to keep the comfort of the way it's always been. Because of these conflicting drives to change and to stay the same, Maloney and Moorefield claim that the key question really is "How can success be achieved and sustained in a healthy, life-enhancing way?"

That's where "one day at a time" comes in. It's gentle enough not to set off the "man the battle stations, something big is trying to force us into being different" part of ourselves. But it does move us into *action*. We're not just sitting around doing nothing. We're doing it—today. However, one day at a time is not an excuse to do it once and then forget it. It requires us to sign on again the next day. And then the next.

Leslie has found this extremely helpful. "I'm six months sober now. I still have dreams about drinking, but as I've learned, if you're dreaming about it, you're not doing it. And as long as I stick to making it through today, my mind leaves me alone about the future." See for yourself.

PRACTICE SELF-APPRECIATION
EVERY DAY

✦ ✦ ✦

If a person focuses on the problem itself and continues to give it powerful mental and emotional energy, [a person] attracts exactly what is
not wanted. By focusing on Gratitude instead, at the same time that the
problem is being confronted, a person connects to Omnipresent, All
powerful, and All knowing Divine Mind and Feeling, and to the heavenly
hosts.

—ANONYMOUS

" I haven't gotten anywhere," Maura moaned the other day about getting upset at work when she'd vowed to keep her cool around her
coworker. But when I pressed her for the facts, it turned out that
she'd stayed calm for most of the past three weeks, getting upset only
once in fifteen days. And rather than exploding at her prickly person,
she walked away and fumed alone. That's a success rate of 93 percent
as measured by getting upset or 100 percent as measured by not blowing up at him. Yet she was acting as if she'd just pulled out a revolver
and shot the guy because one day she felt annoyed at his behavior.

Like Maura, most of us treat ourselves harshly when we stumble—you blew it again, you jerk, can't you ever get it right? So the very least we can do is to recognize and value when we do it right: hey, you managed to keep your cool for the whole week, as you vowed to! Congratulations!

What's so hard about that? In theory, nothing. But in practice, self-appreciation is quite a challenge. At the end of every thinking partner session, I ask the other person and myself to say one thing we appreciate ourselves for in the time we've been together. It's always easy to offer an appreciation to the other person. What's more difficult, I've found, despite having done it thousands of times, is to express gratitude for myself—for my behavior, thoughts, and words in the session. The same is true for everyone I work with. It's much easier to give thanks to someone else than it is to shine the flashlight of appreciation on ourselves. And yet it is so important!

I've been thinking and reading about gratitude for ten years now. So I do know that self-appreciation is powerful stuff. It reinforces the behavior we want to bring into being. It tells the brain: do more of this. So the next time around, you're more likely to make that same good choice.

Being grateful for how we've done has other potent effects. It reminds us that we indeed have succeeded at something we set out to do. When we fail to acknowledge our efforts, it's easy for them to become invisible to us. That's what had happened to Maura. Because she had not stopped to appreciate herself the fourteen days she did it right, she blew out of proportion the one day she (slightly) messed up. She didn't have her successes firmly planted in her mind through appreciation so she lost all perspective.

Recognizing and acknowledging our success also gives us the encouragement to try again tomorrow. Because we are aware of what we've done right, we have more confidence that we can do it again. So when we're grateful for the success we have today, it actually makes it easier to succeed the next day. Especially when it's something that involves a lot of effort over time, it's important to keep appreciating how far you've come. That will give you the energy to keep on.

These emotional effects of gratitude are powerful. For instance, in studies, law students and novice golfers who were asked to pay attention to their positive thoughts (what's right, rather than what's wrong) improved their performance and felt much less stress than those who focused on negative thoughts.

I believe there's more to it than that, though, which is why I included the anonymous quote above. Every human being has three kinds of energy. The first is dynamic, which is the energy of doing. You engage it when you work out, write an action plan, clean your desk. The second is receptive, the energy of not doing. You employ it when you practice patience, listen carefully to someone, relax in a hot tub. The third is magnetic, which is energy that draws toward itself what it wants. You employ it when you set an intention, for instance. When people talk of manifesting something, they are speaking of using magnetic energy.

Gratitude is also magnetic. The more you appreciate something, the more it tends to increase in your life. Why or how this is true is beyond my rational comprehension, but the more I observe, the more I have to conclude that it's true. Focus on problems and they tend to multiply. Focus on what's right and that tends to increase. Notice I say tends to—it's not a direct correlation by any means. We're not totally in charge here. But according to quantum physics, somehow we do increase potentialities with our magnetic thoughts.

Even if you think this is silly, I strongly encourage you to take a moment each day to celebrate the success you're having with your new habit, resolution, or dream. What did you do even a little bit right? The emotional effects of gratitude are well known. And if you increase the possibility of success by drawing toward you more of what you want through the process of gratitude, what's the harm? Either way, by giving thanks today, you'll make your tomorrows more of what you want.

KEEPING GOING

Dreams come true. Without that possibility,
nature would not incite us to have them.

—JOHN UPDIKE

This is the most crucial part of developing a new habit or making a dream come true—sustaining energy and focus over time. It's easy to get swept away with enthusiasm and vow, for instance, to become fluent this year in Chinese, or to never again stress out over the little things. It's another thing altogether actually to live that promise to yourself. In this section, you'll learn the attitudes and behaviors you can adopt to support yourself over time over the long haul, as well strategies for dealing with regret, perfectionism, and folks who want to drag you down. You'll also read about specific ways to handle slip-ups and a process for getting unstuck if you're not seeing enough forward momentum. Remember, your brain physiology is on your side—the more you practice, the easier it's going to get.

HOW YOU GONNA KEEP UP
THE MOMENTUM?

✦ ✦ ✦

No matter how big or soft or warm your bed is,
you still have to get out of it.

—GRACE SLICK

"I've got this problem," says Dolores. "I can set a goal for myself—say, losing ten pounds. And I do it. But then I can't stick with it and the weight comes back on. It's not interesting to me anymore."

Dolores's dilemma reminds me of a story I heard somewhere. There are three groups of people climbing a mountain—social types, competitive types, and achievement types. The social folks have a wonderful time interacting with one another and never get to the top of the mountain. The competitive group fights to see who'll get there first; the winner plants a pole at the top and proclaims, "This is my mountain." Those interested in achievement get to the top and look around and say, "This mountain wasn't so big. Where's the next, bigger one?"

What the story points to is that each of us sustains momentum differently. And one of the keys to creating a lasting change in ourselves is to understand what motivates each of us—what will get us out of bed to do what we promised ourselves—and how to keep it alive for as long as needed.

My sister is, as my mother used to say, "a social butterfly." It's easy for her to exercise when she has someone to do it with because of her desire to connect to others. Dolores is achievement oriented. These people need very challenging goals that are strictly measured and constantly revised upward as each goal is met. If she's trying to exercise regularly, she needs to somehow keep upping the ante herself to stay motivated. Like doing a 5K race, then a 10K—then a triathlon. Ana is motivated by the desire to win. You can get her to learn or do anything by making it a contest in which she can beat someone else.

But those aren't the only momentum creators on the planet. My friend Drew went from a ninety-five-pound weakling type to a buffed-out stud because "he wanted to prove to himself and others that he could." Robin keeps to her diet and exercise plan by "remembering how good eating right and working out makes me feel."

As for me, I keep myself going through my desire for personal integrity. I've developed positive attitudes as well as the habit of exercise because I promised myself I would and I don't want to break my word. I don't want to be a hypocrite. For folks like me, making vows or commitments can be highly effective.

Do you know what works for you to keep your momentum? Setting strict goals and upping the ante? Keeping your word to yourself? Beating someone else?

Knowing what's true for you is crucial. Otherwise, you may end up following someone else's idea of what should work and not finding much success. Here's an example: one of the standard suggestions for keeping momentum is to reward yourself along the way. I personally am not motivated by rewards at all (nor would pasting pictures of skinny models in bikinis on the refrigerator do anything for me except make me depressed). For those who are overeaters or compulsive shoppers, the "reward yourself" idea can even be a dangerous one. That's often the kind of thinking that got them into the predicament in the first place. As Victoria Moran says in *Fit from Within*, "When you lose five pounds, your reward is that you've lost five pounds."

That being said, I once had a client who made a resolution to lose twenty-five pounds and exercise every day for a year. If he kept his promise to himself, he would buy himself a sailboat at the end of the year. You can find him sailing now in the Chesapeake Bay, fit and thin. My husband has been keeping his commitment to work out by "bribing himself," as he puts it. He's been yearning for a new computer. Recently he bought himself one. If he doesn't stick to his fitness plan, he'll have to sell it.

There are no "one size fits all" solutions. If you're not sure what yours are, experiment. Try one suggested here. If that holds no interest, try another. Ask a friend what works for her. But remember—just because it works for her doesn't mean it will for you. Your job is to discover your most effective momentum creator.

WEIGHT LOSS:
"I'M DOING THIS FOR ME"

"After the birth of my son, I was up to 174 pounds," says Brenda Edson. "In 2003, I made a commitment to exercise and eat right and have dropped 42 pounds and kept it off. I exercise pretty much every day and have improved my cholesterol levels, my endurance, and my speed. What worked was to see the weight loss journey as a journey toward a better me, not just a better me in size 4 jeans. I reached a point when I looked at myself and said, "I matter. I'm not doing this to look better. I'm doing this to feel better. I'm doing this for *me*.

"The shift occurred because I became more confident in myself. I think a lot of it was developed on the treadmill. As weird as that sounds, every time I got better or increased my speeds, I gained more confidence in what I could do in the rest of my life. I saw results and I started believing in myself. That confidence let me try new things. I started doing the StairMaster and I started lifting weights, things I was too scared to do before. I just turned thirty-three and I feel better, look better, and have a much better image of myself than ever before."

WHAT'S STANDING IN YOUR WAY?

✦ ✦ ✦

Your compulsive, obsessive, and addictive behaviors each show you frightened parts of your personality. . . . They are your avenues to . . . growth.

—GARY ZUKAV

Ted is a busy executive who decided he wanted to spend more time with his family. He prepared by thinking about why this mattered to him and set a SMART goal (no work two out of four weekends a month and coming home in time to have dinner with the kids three out of five days) and a tracking system—a piece of paper where he marked down when he was there as promised. He's three months into it and he notices that he hasn't even come close to keeping his word to himself. Some work emergency keeps cropping up that forces him to stay late at the office and log weekend hours. He's frustrated with himself. His wife says he needs to be "more committed to the family." I tell him I know he's committed and believe that something else may be going on, something that he needs to get to the bottom of, or it will prevent him from succeeding no matter how hard he tries.

Have you found yourself in a similar dilemma? Not being able to bring what you want into being in any consistent way? Perhaps what's going on is this: while you are truly committed to changing, you're more committed to something else that you are not consciously aware of that prevents you from creating forward momentum.

That's the insight from Robert Kegan and Lisa Laskow Lahey of Harvard University Graduate School of Education. "In the end, the reason New Year's Resolutions . . . have so little power," they write in *How the Way We Talk Can Change the Way We Work,* is that "we are ultimately being disrespectful of our own complexity. We're ignoring the powerful source of [contradictory] behaviors, behaviors that will never change without somehow addressing their source."

For instance, imagine that you say you want to find a long-term relationship and have had no success. It's not that you're not committed to finding a relationship. It's that you're *more* committed to something else—something that contradicts your stated desire but that you believe protects you in some way. For instance, you may be more committed to not getting hurt by anyone ever again than to having a relationship. And underneath that commitment is a core assumption, a belief you formed very early in life that is driving your behavior without your knowledge. For instance, if I am alone I am safe; if I am with someone I will get hurt. You fail to get what you think you want because you haven't gotten to the bottom of it all.

So how do we make visible to ourselves what has been invisible up till now? You'll find a process, adapted from Kegan and Lahey's book, in the box on pages 158 and 159. I used Ted's work life balance situation as an example. I suggest you do the process in writing or with a partner you feel safe with.

You'll know when you've gotten to your core assumption in three ways: First, it's always dire: no one will love you, you'll be abandoned, you'll kill someone, everyone will shun you. Second, in your logical mind, you know it's not true—you aren't going to die if you work out for thirty minutes. But you believe it anyway. You may even feel tears arise. Third, it may have a familiar ring to it. You may think: I've dealt with this in therapy and here it is again, or, I've been to this place before.

As my example showed, Ted realized that, as much as he wanted to be with his family, he was more committed to work because his core belief was that if he ever stopped working, he'd end up destitute. He had come from an economically challenged childhood and feared more than anything being poor again.

As Ted discovered, core assumptions are beliefs we created in childhood to protect us. They represent a child's notion of what we need to do to be safe. They are one of our basic frames; we see the whole world through their lens. We can't just wish or will them away. To break free, we need to, in the words of Kegan and Lahey, "*look at* rather than through" them.

To begin, they suggest that you observe for a week how that assumption shows up in your life. How does it work for you? How does it work against you? For instance, Ted might notice: *Here I am saying yes to more extra work because I am so scared I will lose my job if I say no. I am racing as fast as I can all the time to avoid getting fired.* Next, again without trying to change anything, begin to look for evidence that your assumption is not always true. Because we filter out data that doesn't match our mind-set, we've been ignoring evidence to the contrary for decades. Begin to bring a little factual information into the picture: *Huh, Frank went home early and he still has a job.*

Next, explore the history of your assumption. When did you first think this? What purpose did it serve then? You might discover that what protected you when you were young and vulnerable is standing in your way as an adult: *When I was young, I had no choice but to say yes to any work I could get to help the family.* This awareness hopefully allows us to create compassion for ourselves, to touch the vulnerable part of ourselves with tenderness, rather than judgment or rejection. Whatever our core assumption is, it was our best strategy at the time to deal with our circumstances. We didn't know any other way then. Now, with our adult resources and abilities, we can choose differently.

But it's not a matter of just saying to yourself, okay, make a different choice. You've got to create small tests for yourself to challenge your assumption in a very low-risk way to prove to that younger self that it's okay to let go of this belief. That way you can move from an easy test to a slightly harder one again and again until you have created more and more space for yourself to live beyond your core assumption. For instance, Ted first went home at five one day. Then he took off one weekend. Then he didn't raise his hand to take on more work. By creating experiments and noticing he still had a job, his core assumption relaxed its grip.

For a client trying to let go of perfectionism whose core assumption was that if she made a mistake she would die, I suggested she make a mistake on purpose. Just thinking of doing that was all she could manage for a week. Then she picked something incredibly small—leaving one thing out of place when her best friend came over. Then wearing a shirt with a stain in front of her family. She kept upping the ante until she truly believed she could make a mistake and survive. I knew she'd gotten over the hump when she accidentally forgot a dental appointment and didn't go into a panic.

This is challenging work, which calls on us to grow beyond our previous limitations and bring into the light of our consciousness that which has been driving us our whole lives. Do you see now why I said changing a habit or keeping a resolution was no small endeavor? But the emotional and spiritual payoffs for your inner mining are enormous. Not only will you be more likely to create this particular result, you will have broken free from invisible constraints that have been coloring your view of the entire world.

GETTING TO YOUR CORE ASSUMPTION

1. State your commitment: *I am committed to spending more time with my family.*

2. What are you doing or not doing that's keeping you from realizing your commitment? *Saying yes to any and all work requests so I am rarely home.*

3. What are you afraid would happen if you changed this behavior? *I am afraid that if I don't work eighty hours a week, I will lose my job.*

4. Therefore, what do you want more than being with your family? This is always self-protective—you are protecting yourself from something by your actions or inactions in number 3. *I'd rather have job security than spend time with my family.*

5. State answer number 4 as a countercommitment: *I am more committed to job security than to spending time with my family.*

6. Under the countercommitment is a core assumption that you've believed your whole life. To get at it, ask yourself, what would be so bad if you gave up your countercommitment and met your commitment? *If I don't spend eighty hours at work, I will end up destitute.*

REMEMBER WHAT WILL TRULY
MAKE YOU HAPPY

✦   ✦   ✦

Habits—the only reason they persist is that they are offering some satisfaction. You allow them to persist by not seeking any other, better form of satisfying the same needs. Every habit, good or bad, is acquired and learned in the same way—by finding that it is a means of satisfaction.

—JULIENE BERK

tuned in to *The Biggest Loser* the other day. The show included the initial weigh-in of an obese mother and her sixteen-year-old daughter who was showing signs of adult-onset diabetes and later revealed that she was constantly taunted at school because of her size. The mother weighed in first, at something like 220. As the scales revealed that the daughter was a whopping 251 pounds, the mother burst into tears. "It's my fault," she sobbed. "I just wanted her to do what would make her happy."

My heart went out to this mother. Of course, she had been trying to make her daughter—and herself—happy. That's what all of us are doing. As motivational speaker Sidney Madwed notes, "The motivation for all personal behavior is to produce a sense of 'FEEL GOOD,' a sense of inner peace and well being. . . . This is true whether one signs a million dollar contract, scratches one's nose, rolls over in bed, or just daydreams his life away. People will do things which seem contrary to this concept, but the bottom line is they perceive some kind of payoff which will make them feel good."

Where this mother went wrong is that she confused momentary pleasure with the happiness that comes from health and fitness. She couldn't teach what she didn't know herself. But, stripped down to bra and panties in front of millions of viewers and forced to see the truth about herself and her daughter, she got it. She and her daughter had been pursuing happiness at the end of a fork and had become miserable as a consequence.

But her desire to be happy could become the pathway to liberation. Not without effort, of course. A lot of lettuce leaves, sweat, and time on the treadmill, in their case. But what can keep them going through all the effort is their desire for happiness. The two of them will be happier when they weigh less. Keeping that happiness front and center can help when cravings and the desire to slip back into old habits arise.

This can work for you too. Say your goal is to get out of debt, and a stunning pair of pumps is calling to you from a shop window. You really, really want them. Before you pull out that credit card, pause and ask yourself, What will truly bring me happiness? A new pair of shoes or no debt? If you're still tempted, ask yourself, have all the other pairs I've bought brought lasting happiness?

What you're doing from a brain perspective is engaging your neo-cortex, the thinking brain, rather than your emotional brain. The emotional brain says, "feel good now by having or doing this thing." The thinking brain is the part of us that can say, "Whoa, not so fast. There are consequences to this feel-good-now stuff. Are you going to respect yourself in the morning?"

We all do what we do to feel good. But when our emotional brains are in charge, we damn the consequences and end up suffering later— whether that's through overweight, a hangover, or regret at how we've treated someone. Remembering what brings you real happiness is a technique to keep the thinking brain in charge. That's where what we truly want beyond the temptation of this moment exists.

At the end of *The Biggest Loser* episode I saw, the mother and daughter had lost dozens of pounds; the daughter had no signs of diabetes. Crowed one successful loser, "I feel good for the first time in my life!" Now that's happiness worth having!

LOSING WEIGHT:
"I EAT WHAT I WILL WANT TO HAVE EATEN,
NOT WHAT I WANT TO EAT"

"Fried food is my nemesis," says John Rae-Grant. "As a consequence I was carrying thirty extra pounds of French fries around my gut for the past seven years. One day I decided I had to get serious about weight loss. The first fifteen pounds came off by cutting out fried foods and working out regularly.

"I've now lost over thirty pounds in four months. I eat a lot of sushi and salads. It wasn't even hard during the holidays. I eat what I will want to have eaten, not what I want to eat. Now when I see a plate of French fries and the desire comes up, I think about what I really want—a healthy weight and the ability to keep up with my kids. It's been surprisingly easy."

DON'T LET "THEM" BRING YOU DOWN

✦   ✦   ✦

It never ceases to amaze me: we all love ourselves more than other people, but care more about their opinions than our own.

—MARCUS AURELIUS

Cynthia decided to become a vegetarian, which was considered extremely odd by her boyfriend Scott's mother. "Every time we got together, she would try to make me eat meat. I tried to tell her to back off, which she took offense at. She made scenes at restaurants and told everyone at parties I wouldn't eat what was available, even though I brought my own food and never asked for special treatment. I began avoiding family gatherings, which caused fights between Scott and me."

I've always been flabbergasted, or perhaps the better word is shocked, by people who press drinks on sober alcoholics or cookies on those on a diet. Then there are the dream killers who stomp on your great idea for achieving better work/life balance or ridicule you for becoming a vegetarian.

What is it with such folks? Why doesn't everyone you know applaud and support the changes you're making? Why should they even care? Is the fact that you're evolving threatening in some way? Are they trying to sabotage you?

I don't think it's usually conscious, but we do often threaten those around us when we grow. We could be triggering their insecurity (she won't love me anymore if she's thin) or envy (he's following his dream and I'm not following mine) or challenging their internal excuse that change isn't possible. They may take your healthy change as a judgment against their unhealthy choices. Maybe they need to stop drinking or eating so much as well and they don't want to face that. Perhaps it represents some sacrifice on their part—you've decided to take thirty minutes for yourself every evening and that means they get less attention. There's a host of reasons why they may try to hold you back.

This can be particularly true for those who are nearest and dearest to us. Therapists have known for decades that families are systems and when one part of the system changes, it shakes up the rest. The system then marshals its resources to try to stay the same. None of this is conscious, of course. Almost none of us are aware of the degree to which we take comfort in our fixed ways of being and ideas of ourselves and one another: My mother is the needy one; my brother is the flaky one; I'm the responsible one. She calls me and whines; he always has to be bailed out of trouble. As a consequence of these dynamics, those closest to you may not be eager to support your new choices. They may even actively try to undermine you.

What to do about these naysayers and saboteurs? First, be aware that, as much as you would like it, you may not have support from family and friends. So be sure you do find people who will listen to you and not shame or sabotage—see "What Kind of Support Do You Need?" (page 102). You can ask for family members' and friends' blessing, you can invite them to join you, but you can't make your choices contingent on their behavior. That's a fancy way of saying you mustn't let other people, even those closest to you, determine what you do or how you feel about yourself. You're an adult.

This can be quite challenging if you're someone who looks to others for approval. Heed the words of novelist Lawana Blackwell, "Patterning your life around others' opinions is nothing more than slavery." Take heart—the more you accept responsibility for your choices, the easier it gets. It may even have an overall positive effect on your relationships. When those around you see you unwavering in your commitment, they may grow to respect you.

One great strategy is to be lighthearted about your choice. That's what Cynthia did. "When it became clear Scott and I were headed toward marriage, I knew I had to deal with this differently or else be tortured by his mother forever. I began to make jokes at my own expense— 'here comes the wacky daughter-in-law with the veggie burger to throw on the barbeque.' That helped break the tension."

Cynthia did something else important. She decided to see Scott's mother's comments as a form of caring, even though it didn't feel that way. "I started saying, 'Thank you for being so concerned for my health. I appreciate that you care.' That really did the trick. We got closer and she began to accept my choices. The proof is that five years later, when

I had my daughter and declared I was raising her as a vegetarian, my mother-in-law didn't have heart failure."

Take a tip from Cynthia. You don't need to explain, defend, or justify. Try, "Thanks for your opinion. I'm going to stick to it." And when offered temptations, you only need two words, "No thanks." If they persist, try "I am choosing not to [drink, smoke, eat dessert, etc.]. I'd like you to support me by accepting my no as final." The upside of making assertive statements such as these is that they reinforce your intention and make it easier for you to stick to your commitment to yourself.

Prepare now for what you will do in challenging circumstances with others. That way you won't be put on the spot or get swept away from your good intentions in the tension of the moment. The actress Phylicia Rashad puts it this way: "There's always something to suggest that you'll never be who you wanted to be. Your choice is to take it or keep on moving." Keep moving.

STOPPING NEGATIVE TALK:
"I BEGAN TALKING PEOPLE UP, NOT DOWN"

"Ever feel like you're telling the same negative story over and over?" writes Jessica Yadegaran of the *Contra Costa Times*. "You get together with friends and instead of discussing your health or Australian wines, you analyze—one more time—why John didn't call and how Mary weaseled out of the bill. I realized I was a member of the drama squad when new people joined my circle, bringing with them a lack of knowledge about our sorry stories. Over dinner, while we told a story for the 37th time about an uptight dude who doesn't get the hint, they squirmed in their chairs, twirled their pad Thai and did just about anything short of faking a choke to get through dinner."

As her thirtieth birthday approached, Jessica decided, as one of her birthday intentions, to end her participation in toxic talk. She discovered that as she shifted her own behaviors, her friends followed suit, without her even having to say a word. "Once it hit me, I wiped the dirt off me and swayed the conversation in new directions—to Joe's burgeoning screenwriting career and whether Pam would be good for Jack. I began talking people up, not down." She also began to distance herself from a few folks who didn't take the hint. Now, she tells me, she feels "cleaner, a better person, with more time to talk about the real issues."

USE YOUR ABCDEs ON THOSE NASTY VOICES IN YOUR HEAD

✦ ✦ ✦

Argue for your limitations and sure enough they're yours.

—RICHARD BACH

"I've just realized that I've got a gang of nasty girls inside my head tearing me down," bemoaned Liza one morning. "They're trying to convince me that I will never find a man because I'm too old, too fat, too set in my ways. And the worst thing is that I'm starting to believe them."

What about you? What are the voices inside your head saying? Every one of us has a self-limiting choir that's great at piping up at just the wrong time. Like when you're about to go out on a limb for your dream of becoming a homeowner. Or applying for that job that sounds really great. Or are just about to do the 5K walk. Who needs real naysayers when we've got our own built-in saboteurs who know exactly what to say to bring us down?

Negative self-talk is dangerous to our progress because there is a strong relationship between our thoughts, feelings, and behavior. Negative thinking creates negative feelings, which cause a cascade of stress hormones to be released in our bodies, making it harder for us to produce the positive action we desire. Often these thoughts are not even in our conscious awareness, but are sowing their negative effects regardless.

How to discover and deal with negative self-talk is the subject of countless books. There are hundreds of techniques: imagining a stream, putting each thought on a leaf, and letting it float downstream; envisioning each thought as a ballon that you let go into the sky; saying "thanks for sharing," and moving on; distracting yourself; and so on. One of the most powerful is the ABCDE model of Albert Ellis, who developed rational emotive behavior therapy. It's based on the assumption that once you identify self-limiting beliefs you can dispute or change them. Here's how it works:

A: ACTIVATING EVENT

What made you feel guilty or self-doubting? For example: *I went to the mall yesterday and spent $200 despite promising myself not to buy anything.*

B: BELIEFS

What thoughts do you have about the event? For example: *I have no self-control; I'm never going to change; I might as well give up.*

C: CONSEQUENCES

How do you feel because of your beliefs? For example: *hopeless, de-pressed, angry at myself.*

D: DISPUTE

Challenge the negative beliefs you have identified. Ask yourself if they are completely valid, reasonable, or rational. Start with a phrase like "That's not right," and add a positive statement. For example: *That's not right. I have been doing well for three weeks. I have been keeping my credit card in my wallet as I promised to. I can have control.*

E: EFFECT

How do you feel now that you have challenged your negative thoughts? For example: *I've remembered my successes and so I feel more positive. I think I'll hop into the car and return those things right now.*

Over six thousand research studies have looked at the results of dis-puting negative self-talk statements and replacing them with positive ones and found it to be highly effective in a wide variety of situations. One of the best things we can do for ourselves overall in our lives is to learn to dispute. It's crucially important that you talk back to those voices in your head to counteract their poison.

ANOTHER APPROACH TO DISPUTING

If you have trouble disputing, you might find the work of Byron Katie useful. She changed from a morbidly obese agoraphobic in a halfway house to a renowned and beautiful spiritual guru. Her approach is to help people break free of long-held beliefs that are causing suffering with four questions:

1. Is it true?

2. Can you absolutely know it is true?

3. How do you react when you think that thought?

4. Who would you be without that thought?

Her website offers worksheets and other resources at www.thework.com.

THE IMPERFECT IS OUR PARADISE

✦ ✦ ✦

Fall seven times, get up eight.

—JAPANESE PROVERB

"I 'd been doing so well in communicating better with my mother," wailed Samantha. "And then we had a big blow-up. I'm still furious with her and now on top of it I feel ashamed that I blew my resolution to stay calm around her. But she calls me up and says such insensitive things!"

Although I do know people who have made a resolution and never once slid back, particularly alcoholics and drug users who really got it that they can never use again, most folks blow it from time to time. You just inhaled the whole chocolate cake despite your commitment to eating right. You haven't had a date night with your husband in three weeks, despite vowing to do it weekly. You spiral down into a pit of anxiety over losing your job after promising yourself to look on the bright side.

Many people give up at their first slip-up. "I can't do it," they think. "I'm hopeless." Or, "It's not my fault, the situation is hopeless." Either way, they fall into a puddle of despair and progress stops. That's because they expect perfection.

This harsh standard is the biggest block to getting what we want in our lives. That's why I so love the line by Wallace Stevens: "the imperfect is our paradise." It's the place where our heart's desires become reality, for it is in embracing ourselves just where we are, in all our messy humanity, that we open the doorway to the possibility of transformation.

People who make their dreams come true, who create the results they want in their life, know down to their bones a simple truth. It takes as long as it takes and you may never do it "perfectly." Here's how master teacher Hal Urban puts it in *Choices that Change Lives*: "failure is a fact of life, part of the process. . . . The difference between people who succeed in life and the ones who have difficulty creating success isn't found in the number of times they fail. It's found in the courage they have to take a risk, and it's found in what they do *after* they fail."

Accepting the paradise of the imperfect doesn't mean you give up or ignore what just happened. Rather, it allows you to stop being mired in shame and guilt and try again. At AA, when you fall off the wagon, the next day they remind you that today is now Day 1 of your sobriety. It's another way of saying, okay, you blew it, now get on with it.

Science confirms the power of the imperfect. Studies have shown that dieters who deal constructively with a lapse are more likely to lose weight and keep it off than those who beat themselves up after a mistake.

A friend of mine frames these events as practice: "He's practicing to be sober." "She's practicing being kinder." The more we practice, the better we get. (Statistics show that the average smoker quits four to six times before quitting for good.)

But "practicing" only works if we stop shaming and shoulding ourselves and start paying attention to what the goof-up can teach us about improving our chances for success next time. It clears the mental and emotional haze and allows us to get closer to the mistake to mine it for its wisdom: "I ate the cake because someone brought it for dinner yesterday. I do better when there are no temptations around. From now on, I'm going to ask guests to take their desserts with them when they leave." "Oh, my regular babysitter has been unavailable. I need to find someone else and that might take a while. Meanwhile, I'll suggest to my husband that we have a best friend's night at home after the kids go to bed on Tuesday." "I'm going to make a plan about what to do if I lose my job and then I'm going to think about something else."

When Samantha embraced the paradise of the imperfect, she realized that she'd forgotten what works for her with her mom, which is to think to herself, "She's just saying this because she loves me and this is the only way she knows how, poor woman." She decided to write that sentence by the phone so she could see it every time her mother called. She's doing much better now.

As I write this, the Winter Olympics are ending. The greatest skaters, snowboarders, and skiers in the world just spent two weeks falling down, missing gates, tumbling over themselves and others, then getting up and keeping going. The greatest athletes in the world! My heart leapt at the sight. Not because I'm glad they slipped up, but because I fervently hoped that their example of tenacity and excellence would help banish the notion of perfection forever.

You're good enough as you are to do what you want as well as you can. Just keep at it. In the process, you'll be growing your soul as well as a new behavior. You'll be learning how to be gentler to yourself and others as you live with the rest of us in the paradise of the imperfect.

YOU CAN'T CHANGE WHAT YOU'VE DONE, ONLY WHAT YOU'RE GOING TO DO

✦ ✦ ✦

Don't get hung up on a snap in the stream, my dear. Snaps alone are not so dangerous—it's the debris that clings to them that make the trouble. Pull yourself loose and go on.

—ANNE SHANNON MONROE

was going great guns on my exercise routine. Then I got sick and fell behind on my book deadline. After I dragged myself out of bed, I hunkered down in front of the computer. As a result, in the past thirty days, I've kept my resolution of daily exercise seven times.

They say confession is good for the soul but I feel embarrassed. Who am I to be writing a book about sticking to a resolution? Okay, so I no longer expect perfection from myself. But this is so far off the mark that I am entertaining serious notions of canceling my gym membership and deleting this piece so you won't know I failed.

I've got to find a way to go on. Flicking through the TV channels, I come across *The Suze Orman Show* and hear her say to someone: "You can't change what you've done, only what you're going to do." Thank you, Suze. It's just the message I need in order to not get hung up in regret and "if onlys," and to decide what I'm going to do now to begin again.

But before I jump into action, I've got to do something to renew my trust in myself. Otherwise my emotional brain is going to continue to sabotage my efforts with feelings of hopelessness. I made a commitment to myself I have not kept. If I did that to anyone else, I would apologize. Why shouldn't I treat myself with equal respect?

I was fifty-three before I learned the steps to a good apology (see the Self-Apology box). It's not a matter of just saying "I'm sorry." It's a process of learning from your mistake and restoring trust, in this case, in yourself. I encourage you to try this process of apology if you break your commitment. Apologizing to yourself is very powerful. It acknowledges that you take your resolution seriously. It allows you to treat yourself and your goals with the utmost respect. And it allows you to learn from what happened so that you can improve.

You can't change what you've done. For the past two weeks, I chose to write like a madwoman from 5 A.M. to 8 A.M., then talk to clients all day, make dinner, and fall into bed by 9. But I can change what I'm going to do. I will stop as soon as I finish working on this piece and take the dog for a walk before the sun sets. I can't change the past. But apologizing to myself makes it easier for me to change the future.

SELF-APOLOGY

There are four parts:

1. Acknowledge the commitment that wasn't kept: *I said I was going to exercise every day and I've only done it seven times this month.*

2. Describe the consequences of breaking your commitment: *As a result, I have less faith in myself and it's harder to believe I can do it.*

3. Remember your context not as an excuse but as a way of learning: *I was sick for two weeks and had two other writing projects with pressing deadlines that popped up besides the book.*

4. Explore what will restore trust: *Remembering the context of all that I've been doing helps me see it's not because I'm lazy or untrustworthy that I haven't worked out. In the future, when I get sick, I will make sure to renegotiate my deadlines so that I can give myself some breathing room.*

SIFT WHEN YOU WANT TO GIVE UP

✦ ✦ ✦

There are two voices in your head—one is always wrong.

—KAREN CASEY

gave up drinking Coke a couple months ago. A can a day was one of my principal vices. Once, on a strict vegetarian retreat, a friend and I escaped into town. She was dying for a glass of red wine. I wanted my Coke fix. As I am otherwise caffeine and sugar free, I drank it to get me going some early mornings or as a pick-me-up at midafternoon when I still had a slew of clients to talk to. It was my treat to look forward to, my reward for working hard. But now that I know how much exercise it takes to burn off those 140 calories every day, I've sworn off.

I still have cravings. At random moments every day, a little voice in my head still says, "Wouldn't a cold coke with ice and fresh lemon be great right now?" Desire rises up strongly. I can't even imagine how much stronger the cravings must be for people who are physically addicted to alcohol and cigarettes or other drugs.

What I've learned, however, is that if I don't give in, if I just hang on for a bit, the desire passes. Scientists tell us that on average cravings attack four to seven times a day and last only seconds. So what we really need are strategies for mere seconds.

This fleetingness is also a crucially valuable insight from Buddhism—that thoughts and feelings rise and then they pass away. You don't have to act upon them, you don't have to cling to them, you don't have to push them away. They simply arrive and at some point they will disappear. The more we pay attention to the *process* of rising and passing, the less hooked we are by the *content* of our thoughts and feelings.

Addiction experts call this "urge surfing." Here's how Susan Nolen-Hoeksema, Ph.D., puts it in *Eating, Drinking, Overthinking*: "Urges behave like waves—they start small, build to a crest, then break up and dissolve. When you urge surf, you ride the wave rather than fight it; as a result, you are less likely to be pulled in or wiped out."

Want to learn how to urge surf? It's very simple but counterintuitive. We've been taught to run from or give in to strong feelings. This requires doing the opposite. As soon as you become aware of a strong sensation, rather than ignore or indulge it, you turn and pay *more* attention to it. The box accompanying describes one way to do this called SIFT. SIFT is a three-minute process that stands for Sensation, Image, Feeling, Thought. It's useful not only for urges, but for any strong feeling—fear, sadness, anger, inertia, worry, despair. Neuroscientists say that it helps balance us because it uses both sides of the neocortex and helps reduce amygdala hijacks, those takeovers of our thinking brains by our emotional ones.

To SIFT, you must differentiate between thoughts, images, feelings, and sensations. "I want a Coke" is a thought. Desperation is a feeling.

The picture of you being deprived is an image. What most of us are least aware of is our bodily sensations associated with our thoughts and feelings. Where exactly are the sensations in your body? Where are they located—in your mouth? Your stomach? Your head? Describe them as if you were a newspaper reporter and could not use any words except precise descriptions without interpretations: it's a hot tingly sensation centered in my throat that pulses in and out. Focus your attention on the sensation. Does it move? Vary in intensity? How far inside is it? How far does it spread? Is it anywhere else in your body? Give the sensations the kind of curious attention you would give someone you'd just met and were intrigued with. The idea is to recognize what you are experiencing, without trying to change it.

SIFT is an awareness practice that strengthens our "witness self," or what Buddhist monk Thich Nhat Hanh calls our blue-sky mind. Our thoughts and feelings are like the clouds that race across the sky. Even when it's obscured by clouds, the blue sky is always there. From the blue sky perspective, all is calm. Serene even.

I like to think of this blue-sky mind as my best or highest self. That's where what I really want resides. I want to make sure that's the mind in the driver's seat or else I can be blown off course by my habitual mind with its clouds of attachment (I want it now and damn the consequences) or aversion (I absolutely can't stand this for a second more). That's why I love the opening quote from recovery expert and former alcoholic Karen Casey. She reminds us that we can't trust the mind that leads us into temptation or negative habits. What we can trust is that our feelings and thoughts will change and that we don't have to act on them. Or not act because of them.

I've done this with hundreds of folks in all kinds of feeling states and usually, after a few minutes of focused attention, the sensation ebbs. Sometimes it gets stronger first. But eventually, it diminishes. It's as if all the feelings and thoughts we've ever been afraid of or run from or given in to are nothing but tantruming two-year-olds desperate for attention. If we simply sit down and really pay attention for a few minutes, they quiet down.

This process works—but it's not a "done-that-now-what?" thing. Depending on what you're changing, how much fear you must walk through, or how often cravings arise, you may find the need to SIFT several times a day. There have been brief times in my life when I've used it hourly. It takes a bit of bravery—to turn toward rather than away from that which is appearing to torment you. Hopefully the relief you experience once you try it will make it easier the next time you need it.

SIFT IN THE FACE OF STRONG FEELINGS

Sensations: What are the sensations in my body? (*heat, cold, pressure, constriction, expansion*) Where are they located?

Images: What images are coming up? (*myself curled in a ball, a blank wall, a plane crashing*).

Feelings: What emotions am I experiencing? (*fear, sadness, anger, lethargy, hopelessness*).

Thinking: What are the stories I'm telling myself? (*I can't survive, this will never end, I will always be alone*).

The point is to recognize what's going on inside of you so that you don't have to act upon it.

HAVE A LITTLE FUN WITH IT, WILL YOU?

✦　　✦　　✦

Humor is by far the most significant activity of the human brain.

—EDWARD DE BONO

Patrick began to learn about nutrition when one of his sons was diagnosed with food allergies. He was the typical Midwestern McDonald's hamburger and French fries guy. Now, he says, "I spend so much money at Whole Foods, the corporate office knows me by my first name." But he's not a fanatic. "I could only learn to eat healthy because I found ways for it to be fun and interesting. I love cooking and eating all this new stuff. But if I took it too seriously, I'd get bored and feel deprived. I still have my little indulgences, like nonfat soymilk lattes at Starbucks. And I poke fun at myself at work for eating weird things. But coworkers see what I look like and come up privately to ask about things like tofu and quinoa."

Lynn is a young assistant professor of archaeology. She has a full teaching load, is knee deep in her own research, has a set of graduate students she's advising, and is trying to get enough publications to assure her tenure. Despite that workload, she manages to exercise every day. "I couldn't do it until I found activities I love to do—swim and play squash. I enjoy both so much that they are like little islands of enjoyment in the middle of my day. Making it fun has been my secret to success."

Are you having fun yet? I think of fun in two ways. First there's the possibility of actually enjoying the new habit itself. That's especially easy when we've chosen something potentially fulfilling—learning the two step, getting to know your new neighborhood, getting the pile of papers off your desk, following your dream of getting a pilot's license. The more you can find ways to make your new habit fun, the more likely you'll stick to it. Do it with friends, create a contest with your kids to see who's better at it, make it into a silly game.

But there's another kind of fun you can have, no matter what you've chosen. And that's lightening up around the goal itself. Stop taking yourself so seriously. Intention and determination are wonderful, but they work better when mixed with a dash of self-deprecating humor. When I'm about to lose my cool, for instance, I like to tease myself into better behavior by imagining the headline in the *National Enquirer*: AUTHOR OF BOOK ON PATIENCE BLOWS OUT HUSBAND'S BRAINS FOR FAILURE TO REMEMBER WHAT SHE SAID 30 MINUTES AGO. That puts me back on track in a lighthearted way.

Remember—our emotional brains want fun. I was reminded of this recently when my bride-to-be client was complaining to me how hard it was to keep from bickering with relatives over the wedding plans. "Have a little fun with it," I recommended. "Enlist your fiancé to help relieve the pressure. Turn it into a reality show: 'Wedding Survivor.' Or play 'Guess Who'll Pitch a Fit Next over Not Being Allowed to Invite Cousin Louie.' Laughing about it will allow you to more easily keep your intention to stay calm."

We take ourselves and our problems so very seriously. We use our willpower and our won't power. Don't forget to use a little wit power as well.

ASK FOR HELP FROM INVISIBLE HANDS

✦　✦　✦

Think of yourself as an incandescent power, illuminated and perhaps
forever talked to by God and his messengers.

—**BRENDA UELAND**

I would characterize my friend Rick as a devout atheist. So it was with
astonishment that I listened to him tell me about an experience he
once had. "I was sitting in a meditation retreat and in a lot of physical pain. I wasn't sure I could sit any longer. Then I remembered something my teacher Joseph Goldstein had said. That there are all kinds of
Buddhas and devas in other realms who will help us if we call on them.
So I did and the pain instantly went away." I remembered Rick's words
years later when I was working with Sombofu Some, of the Dagara tribe
in West Africa, who told me, "The ancestors are there, always ready to
help us if we ask."

Both of these incidents came back to me recently as I was interviewing Gina, an alcoholic who has been sober for twenty years. "I had tried
many times before to stop but always the cravings got the best of me,"
she explained. "Then my doctor told me my liver was showing damage

and I tried again. When I went to AA, I told my sponsor how afraid I was of the cravings. 'Get down on your knees and pray to God to take the cravings away,' she advised. I did and I never had even one."

God, ancestors, Buddhas, and devas . . . Every culture has a belief in some sort of higher power or "invisible hands," as Joseph Campbell names it, a spiritual force that wants the best for us and will come to help if we but request it. I'm not sure where I stand, but I do honor that multitudes of human beings have received great aid and comfort from a spiritual source. And I do know that sometimes, when the going gets tough, all any of us can do is throw up our hands and cry "This is beyond me." It's the first step in all the twelve-step programs that have helped so many millions of people change for the better. That should be a clue that it might be useful in whatever you're working on too.

I remember seeing a therapist once who advised me to pray for help in finding a love relationship that would last. "How do I go about praying?" I asked. "Open your mouth and yell 'help!'" he responded.

That's really all you have to do. Ask for help: Help me keep my temper with my son. Help me find the good in today. Help me choose the right business partners. Help me eat healthily. Help me learn to include myself in my caretaking. Whatever it is that you are working on, ask for help from invisible hands. You don't have to understand or believe. How or why it works, like everything in the spiritual realm, is a mystery to us on the human plane.

Oh yeah, one more thing. Don't forget to accept the help that may turn up. Don't be like the guy in the old joke who's sitting on top of his house in a flood, asking God to save him. Along comes a rowboat with two men who offer to take him. "Nope," he replies, "I'm waiting for God to save me." The water gets higher. Soon a helicopter comes by. "I'm waiting for God," the man says. Eventually the floodwaters overtake the house and the man drowns. He finds himself in front of God. "I prayed to you. Why didn't you save me?" he demands. "I sent a boat and then a helicopter," replies God. "What more did you want?"

YOU DON'T HAVE TO SCARF DOWN
THE WHOLE BOX JUST BECAUSE YOU
ATE ONE COOKIE

✦   ✦   ✦

The most difficult matter is not so much to change the world
as yourself.

—NELSON MANDELA

t's Week 12 of my no Coca-Cola resolution. You know how it goes—
I'd been doing pretty well but then hit a few bumps. I was traveling
for two weeks, which required waking up in different time zones and
having to be "on" early each day. I needed a caffeine boost to get going
and relied on a Coke to do it. Then two. Then . . .

Have you ever succumbed to the "I just ate one cookie so I might as
well eat the whole box" syndrome? It doesn't have to be about food—it
could be one cigarette, one moment of explosive rage, one attack of fear
of taking that business risk, one day of missing the gym. Anything that
causes us to do what we've sworn we won't do or not do what we've
promised ourselves we will. We're so mad at ourselves for violating a

rule that we punish ourselves by abandoning all control. We indulge even more in the forbidden substance or rage even louder at our spouse. Or get even more paralyzed by fear. Or decide we might as well give up because we've missed one day.

Psychologists call this the abstinence violation effect. It's a result, they say, of a harsh all-or-nothing attitude toward our behavior. It's paradoxical—the more we hold ourselves to a rigid standard, the more we then abuse ourselves with the very thing we've outlawed when we blow it. Here's how Susan Nolen-Hoeksema, explains it in *Eating, Drinking, Overthinking*: "When you set absolute rules for yourself that are highly likely to be violated, and then you do violate them, you feel bad about yourself and sink into depression. Then you may eat or drink [or give in to other negative behaviors] to escape from that feeling." Sound familiar?

It doesn't have to be that way. One way around the abstinence violation effect is to know in advance that there will be times you will blow it. You won't stick to your organizational routine, you won't take a chance to speak to the cute guy at the coffee shop, you will blow off practicing your language tapes, you will get caught up in perfectionism again . . .

Whatever it is that you're learning, somewhere along the way you'll blow it. Guaranteed. Know why? It's not because you're weak or stupid or undisciplined. Psychologists James O. Prochaska, John C. Norcross, and Carlo C. DiClemente, who have been studying change for over twenty years, say it's because what they call relapse (a temporary fall back into old ways) is an inevitable part of the change process. It simply goes with the territory. The more you understand and really embrace the truth of that, the fewer negative consequences there will be when you blow it. Blowing it doesn't mean you have to punish yourself in overindulgence. It just means that today you relapsed. Tomorrow you can make another choice.

That's what I did about my Coke problem. In the past, I would have said after the first one, "Well, I've blown it now so I might as well have three—or go back to drinking one every day." But this time, I allowed myself the one Coke and the next day went back to my resolution. As a result, out of sixty-six days, I have had six Cokes. Not bad, really. Certainly better than the sixty-six or more I would have had by now if I had given in to the abstinence violation effect.

Those who study this phenomenon say that the best thing to do is to prepare for lapses. Recognize *now* that you may have slip-ups and commit to not giving up. What is it that you want to remember when you have a lapse? Write it down and pull it out when you need it. Here's mine: "I commit to not drinking Coke but if I slip up and do, it's not the end of the world. I can make a better choice tomorrow."

At the deepest level, avoiding the abstinence effect requires you grow your capacity for self-forgiveness, the ability to compassionately let yourself off the hook of condemnation and self-hatred when you make a mistake. Many of us think that forgiveness is just a way of letting ourselves fail without consequences. But it's actually the opposite. Forgiving ourselves for relapses keeps us from self-punishment that actually causes us to compound the error—eating the whole loaf because you had one bite.

Self-forgiveness will keep you from hurting yourself more by bathing you in the balm of loving-kindness. But it will also increase your compassion for others. It's been my experience with clients that those who are the harshest with themselves also hold others to impossible standards. The ropes of judgment that imprison us with unrealistic expectations also keep us from embracing other human beings. When we practice forgiveness of our own foibles and failings, we cultivate the capacity to do the same for those around us who need our loving care. We expand the capacity of our hearts.

So when you blow it, as you most likely will, please forgive yourself and move on. As William Durant counsels, "Forget past mistakes. Forget failures. Forget everything except what you are going to do now and do it." You'll be growing your soul as well as your capacity to change this particular way of being.

LOOK AT THE CHARACTER STRENGTHS YOU'RE CULTIVATING

✦   ✦   ✦

Your beliefs become your thoughts. Your thoughts become your words.
Your words become your actions. Your actions become your habits. Your
habits become your values. Your values become your destiny.

—MAHATMA GANDHI

Ana's favorite subjects, she tells me, are lunch and recess. She tends to rush through her schoolwork to get done as quickly as possible. The upside, as the teacher pointed out, is that she's not afraid to make a mistake. The downside is that she makes careless errors. So the new habits she's been working on this year are checking her answers and being more thorough.

In helping her, I've realized that, as with all of us, this is about something more than getting the answers right on the third-grade science test. It's about developing character strengths that she can use throughout her life—persistence and thoroughness and striving for personal excellence. And when I work with her on being more thorough, it helps her to see it in this larger context. Because frankly, she and I both know that whether she checks Tuesday's math problems doesn't matter in the big scheme of things. It's the cultivation of the character strengths the checking represents that matters. When I help her focus on *that*, the redoing of her math, the expanding of her persuasive paragraph, is easier.

The same may be true for you. Of course you want to lose those forty pounds, quit your job and start over, get out of debt, or whatever your new habit is. Those are worthy goals that will reap specific rewards — greater health, more meaningful work, less financial stress. But, as you know, the work of actually reaching them can be tedious, boring, fear-creating, challenging, or any number of other unpleasant adjectives. By paying attention to the positive qualities of heart and mind that you are developing as a result of sticking to your goal, you give yourself greater incentive to hang in there.

What are the character strengths you've been cultivating as you work this change? The capacity to say no to harmful impulses (self-regulation)? The awareness that you can rely on your own word (self-trust)? The ability to pick yourself up and begin again, no matter how many times (resilience)? Determination to succeed? Humor? Compassion? Humility? Patience? Forgiveness? Courage? All of the above?

In many ways, developing these qualities is the real reward of change. To my mind, they are more important than your resolution itself because they are transferable. These attributes and others like them are the ones we need in order to create meaningful and satisfying lives, the two building blocks of happiness.

That's why I say changing anything in ourselves, no matter how small, is a powerful act. Through it, we grow aspects of ourselves we would not otherwise develop. That is because character strengths are formed only through some kind of challenge, a rising above our previous limitations.

Here's what Brenda Edson, who lost forty-two pounds and has kept them off through exercise and eating right, has to say about the qualities she's cultivated: "What I developed was drive, an inner determination to make it work. Failure wasn't an option for me. Persistence too. I had to develop that. There are times when I have setbacks. The difference is that I now look at it in the long term. If I make a mistake, I forget about it and move forward.

"I gained courage as well. Courage to look at myself honestly and objectively. Courage to make these drastic changes in my life. Courage to ignore all of those well-meaning people who said, 'Oh, one bite of cake won't hurt. You look fine.' I can't think of another word that describes it any better. I had to find the fight and fire in myself to get on that treadmill and to make my body sweat, to make my muscles burn. Another quality was strength. I would never have described myself as strong before I made these changes in my life. But now, I know that I have an inner strength that will keep me going, even when it's not so easy.

"The end result is that I found something deep down within me that I never knew existed. I found that fire and that determination that has helped me through times of stress and crisis. I found that drive that keeps me going and makes me believe that I can be a better person every single day."

Take a few moments to write down what qualities you've grown in yourself with this change. It's a way of acknowledging your efforts and inspiring you to keep on going. Now how are you going to celebrate your newfound qualities? They are your true treasures, and can never be taken away.

RUNNING A MARATHON:
"MY GOAL IS TO SUCCEED"

"Jafet Perez used to run the streets of East Oakland, tagging buildings and breaking into cars," writes Janine DeFao in the *San Francisco Chronicle*. Then, at sixteen, he got hooked up with a program called Students Run Oakland, which helps turn at-risk kids around by training them for marathons. Despite being expelled from school, Jafet trained and completed the 2005 marathon in four hours, fourteen minutes. "I like the competition, the cheers, everyone saying you can do it," he told the *Chronicle*. He hopes to break a record in the 2006 marathon and declares that the discipline he developed from running has given him the confidence to enroll in continuation school to get his high school diploma. "I need to get out from the streets and get my mind on something else. My goal is to succeed in life and stop joking around."

ONCE YOU CREATE THE NEW HABIT, IT'S YOURS FOR LIFE

✦　✦　✦

We are the choices we make.

—MERYL STREEP

atthew is a high-performance executive who came to work with me to get better at relationship building. His habit was to get into the office, shut his door, put down his head, and plow through what he considered his "real" work. But he'd recognized that to be truly excellent, he needed to get out from behind his desk and interact more with employees, bosses, vendors, and business partners. He had recognized the importance of such "fluffing and tending," as I call it, and had been working on it for six months.

"I may never like it," he admitted, "but I must say it's definitely paid off—that contract negotiation went smoothly because I spoke to both sides unofficially. And it's getting easier. Each Friday afternoon when I look at what I've done, I notice that I've actually spoken to all the people on my list more often than not. I don't have to force myself so hard and don't forget so often."

"Congratulations," I replied. "You've created a new habit! And here's the really good news—once you've done something enough times to make a new neural pathway, it's there for life. What that means is that you've gone from having to make a conscious effort to it being fairly automatic. You don't have to work so hard anymore to get the results you want. In the change process, you're now officially in the maintenance stage."

If you follow the suggestions in this book, at some point you'll be there too. Exactly when depends on the complexity of what you set out to do, how deeply entrenched the old habit is, and how often you practice the new one. As Gary Zukav says in *The Mind of the Soul*, "Choice equals creation . . . You are the artist and you are also the art being created."

How do you know when you've gotten there? It's an important question. Remember, it doesn't necessarily mean you're perfect every time. Rather, like Matthew, you succeed more often than not and you don't have to work so hard to remember. When you get off track, it's easier to get back on. That means you've created the groove in your brain that you've been working toward.

It's important to recognize when you've gotten to this point so that you can stop and appreciate yourself. It's easy to focus on when you *haven't* done things right or where you want to go *next*. We are all experts in keeping ourselves in a perpetual state of dissatisfaction. But it's crucially important that you stop, acknowledge your progress, and celebrate your success. You've done it! You set out to lose weight or become less stressed or create better friendships or get your financial house in order, whatever it was that you wanted. And through the positive choices you made and all the work you did, you've created a healthy new habit that can be yours for life.

This is no small thing—remember, most people who make resolutions fail. If you don't take the time to celebrate your success, your brain won't register you've done it. And you won't be able to reap all the rewards of learning. For you haven't just learned to do this particular thing. By stopping and asking yourself questions such as How did I do it? What helped the most? What didn't work? What did I do to get back on track when I got discouraged or blew it? you stockpile valuable information about how to do anything else you might want.

This has been a journey not only of weight loss or becoming happier or more organized. It has been nothing less than an exploration of your heart and soul. You've had to find something positive to go toward that you really want, you've learned to relate to the scared parts of yourself in a different way, you've developed qualities such as persistence and willpower, you've learned how not to give in to the impulses of the behaviors you no longer want, you've developed compassion and the ability to forgive yourself. These are precious resources.

So please, take a moment now to appreciate yourself, to recognize how far you've come and what you've learned along the way. If you were complimenting a friend, what would you say? Would you be willing to write yourself a congratulations note and read it out loud? I will if you will. Behavior we celebrate grows ever stronger.

LESS STRESS: "I FINALLY FEEL FREE"

"Since high school, I was your classic overachiever," says Alan. "By the time I was thirty-three, I was an assistant professor at an Ivy League college. Papers, students, research, guest lectures . . . I was racing eighteen hours a day. Then my world came crashing down when I hurt my back. I could not move, period. First I tried to gut it out, but finally I realized I had to change my work habits. I had only a set amount of time and energy. I learned to prioritize, let go of all that didn't have to get done, and put my own health and well-being on my radar screen. I started to exercise (slowly) and to ask myself when a new opportunity came along, "What am I willing to let go of to do this?" I've been at it for nine months now and not only am I physically in good shape, but I finally feel free of the hamster wheel I'd been whirling on for most of my life. I realized I can say no and not only survive, but thrive."

THE OLD PATHWAY'S STILL THERE TOO
—BEWARE OF STRESSORS

✦   ✦   ✦

Every habit he's ever had is still there in his body, lying dormant like flowers in the desert. Given the right conditions, all his old addictions would burst into full and luxuriant bloom.

—MARGARET ATWOOD

Everyone knows the story of Peter Jennings, who stopped smoking for many years and then began again in the stress of 9/11. His is a sadly cautionary tale that has to do with how our brains are structured.

Like Peter when he was not smoking, by now you've practiced your new habit—eating right, better decision making, risk taking in relationships, less clutter—enough that you've created a new pathway in your brain. That means it's easier for you to do it. It doesn't take as much effort or as many reminders. Cravings have subsided. It may even be automatic, meaning you don't have to think about it. You just go to the gym after work, are calm around the in-laws who used to drive you insane, are well launched into your new relationship, leave the office by six-thirty most evenings, don't have to think every minute about not pulling out the credit card. Life is good!

Then something happens—you switch jobs and your routine changes dramatically. Suddenly you're back to eating Ho-Hos and vegging out on the couch. An office crisis arises and all the hard-won balance you've achieved gets blown as you work eighteen-hour days. Fred forgets to call to say he's going to be late and you respond by calling off the wedding and moving out. Your mother dies and you go on a spending spree. What's happened? Psychologists call it "instinctual drift," the tendency to go back to the old habit.

But why? Because the pathway to your old behavior is still there in your brain. Scientists tell us that the neurons that fire together wire together (meaning they are likely to fire that way the next time) and you've fired that particular sequence so many times that it ain't going away. Don't lose heart—remember that you've created a new pathway through your hard work and that's there too.

Think of the two options as parallel roads. As long as you go down the new road, you'll get the results you want. But stress can cause your car to jump the tracks and travel down the old road in the blink of an eye.

Psychologists call the ability to live up to our intentions the capacity for self-regulation, also known as good old-fashioned self-control. They've studied it extensively and what they've learned can really help us stay away from the old road. First, they compare self-regulation to a muscle that gets depleted after use. That's because studies have shown that it's much harder to stick to your intention when you've just had to use self-control in some other area. It's also easier in the morning, they've discovered, when you're fresh, than in the evening when your capacity has been depleted. That's why AA, Weight Watchers, and other support groups teach members to HALT: that is, to be particularly careful when Hungry, Angry, Lonely, or Tired.

Okay, so we're supposed to get lots of rest and avoid stress to husband our capacity for self-control. But not many of us get to completely control the stress level in our lives. We can try to manage and minimize it, but sometimes life just throws us a big old curve.

This is a situation where information is power. By identifying what causes you stress, you can come up with alternatives before you go off the rails. For instance, I know that under deadline pressure, I sacrifice my exercise routine. Fearful of not finishing on time, I want to use every minute for writing. Once I'm aware of this pattern, I can make compromises with myself at the beginning of the day: you can skip the gym, which takes the better part of an hour, if this evening, after you're too tired to work, you dance with Ana and Don for twenty minutes. What can you plan in advance to deal with the stress you'll most likely encounter?

Of course, we can't plan for every eventuality. But by understanding why we blow it under stress, we can treat ourselves kindly and not make matters worse. It's not because you're weak. It's a function of brain physiology. Cut yourself some slack, then read the next chapter. You'll get some other practical tips for getting back on track.

WHEN BLOWN OFF COURSE,
APPLY THE FOUR As

✦　✦　✦

It's never too late, in fiction or in life, to revise.

—NANCY THAYER

You'd been doing well and then something threw a monkey wrench into your formula for success. For Oprah, her latest weight gain was caused, if I remember correctly, by her sudden inability to run due to knee problems. For Tracy, a client, it was her company's budget crisis. She suddenly had to put in many long evenings and weekends finding ways to cut expenses, which interfered with her intention to achieve better work/life balance. For me it was my gym going out of business three weeks before Christmas. Between the busyness of the holidays (I didn't have time to look for someplace new) and holiday parties, I woke up on January 2 carrying a significant amount of extra weight.

Make no mistake—setbacks suck. You're right back where you started. Actually it's worse, because you've set off that part of your mind that whispers, "See, you can't do this. Just give up. Give in. It's not worth even trying." This is a truly dangerous moment. Because if we listen to this voice, not only do we not change this time, but we decrease the possibility of ever changing because we lose faith in ourselves.

That's why when circumstances throw us off course, as they inevitably will, it's time for the Four As:

1. Assess the current situation.

2. Adjust what needs to be done.

3. Admire yourself for having the strength to start again (a strategy of fitness guru Bob Greene).

4. Act quickly to implement your new course of action.

For instance, Oprah assessed her knee problems, found a new exercise routine, was able to admire herself for her ability to start over (since Greene has been her trainer presumably he taught her how to do this), and put her revised plan into action. Now she's once again in great shape and back to a healthy weight. Tracy saw that her work crisis would be over in one month. She adjusted her expectation that she would have time for her family in those four weeks, admired herself for being willing to try again, and decided that at the end of four weeks, she'd take Friday afternoons off again. I found a new gym and devised a plan of more vigorous exercise and a better diet.

To my mind, the most important As are the last two. Admiring ourselves helps us stay positive and avoid a spiral into negative self-esteem—"Oh see, I'm not capable of doing this right. This slip-up proves it." It turns a mishap into an esteem boost when we remind ourselves that it takes great courage and persistence to not give up.

Acting quickly is also crucial. Otherwise, we'll lose the energy of our commitment and slide back into our bad old behaviors. Hopefully you've created contingency plans, as I suggested in Part III. Perhaps you can get one of those going now. I'd known my gym was closing but had done nothing to search for a new one. It never occurred to me that it would take time to find the right one or that it would close over the holidays when I had little time for the search.

Perhaps this setback is something that never occurred to you—your mother is moving in with you, your husband lost his job—so you have no Plan B. That's where assessment and adjustment come in. What's nonnegotiable is that you're doing your thing. *How* and *when* you're going to do it—that's what's open to all kinds of rearrangements.

Keeping this awareness in the face of setbacks is key. I remember a friend coming to visit for a few days and asking me where the closest gym was. While the rest of us sat around in the mornings talking, she would take off for an hour. At the time, I thought she was a bit of a fanatic. Now I honor her ability not to let traveling set her back. And you should see how fabulous she looks at age fifty.

Remember, even Oprah has had to pick herself up and start again many times—in front of millions, no less. So when blown off course, get the four As in gear. It doesn't matter how many times you begin again. It only matters that you begin again.

Become an expert at starting over—you'll not only make your dream come true but increase your self-esteem, self-respect, and self-confidence.

TWELVE TIPS FOR KEEPING YOUR PROMISE TO YOURSELF

1. MAKE IT NONNEGOTIABLE

Promise yourself that you are absolutely going to do it. When you do it, where you do it, how you do it can, and most likely will, change according to circumstances. But *that* you will do it is not open for consideration. Call it a vow, a promise, a pledge, a commitment. Whatever you name it, making it choiceless is a tool for overcoming backsliding after your initial enthusiasm fades. You don't negotiate with yourself about brushing your teeth. You just do it. I bet you usually honor your commitments to other people too. Treat yourself equally well. Make your resolution a nonnegotiable commitment in your life.

2. MAKE IT ACTIONABLE

Is your goal concrete enough? Many of us fail because we haven't turned it into something to actually do. Yesterday, a client said he was going to focus more on himself and his family and less on his job. "How are you going to put that into action?" I asked. There was silence on the other end of the phone. Here are some resolutions I've recently heard: to have more energy . . . to learn to relax . . . to learn to make decisions. There's nothing wrong with these desires. But they must be translated into actions. Actions tell you *how* you're going to do something—I'm going to go to bed earlier and exercise thirty minutes daily to have more energy; I'm going to spend a half hour a day relaxing with my feet up on the couch; I'm going to make a decision about the vacation by Friday. To succeed you *must* know what actions you're going to take.

3. COME UP WITH SOLUTIONS FOR YOUR USUAL EXCUSES

What is your usual litany of excuses and rationalizations? One way to think about this is to ask yourself what has gotten in your way in the past when you've tried to keep this resolution or any other. Forgetting? No time? Losing interest? Not knowing how to begin? And what are the rationalizations you give yourself when you gave up in the past? It doesn't matter? It's not that bad? It's too hard? Instead of just hoping it will be different this time, write down your typical excuses and rationalizations and create strategies in advance for dealing with them. That way you won't get stopped in your tracks and lose forward momentum when they arise. And yes, they will! Because of the way our brains are wired, we have a strong tendency to repeat behavior over and over.

4. USE PROCRASTINATION TO YOUR ADVANTAGE

Business coach Mike R. Jay claims that 60 percent of the population is "pressure prompted," as it's called on the Myers-Briggs Type Indicator. It's a preference, usually labeled as procrastination, for taking in information for as long as possible before being forced into action by some external deadline. The other 40 percent of us are "early starters," who prefer to get the ball rolling and avoid pressure. If you fall into the pressure-prompted majority, find a deadline that will help you get into motion—a reunion, a vacation, a wedding, a performance. One would-be dieter and exerciser finally got off the starting line when he got the lead in a local production of *The Full Monty*, which required him to parade around in a g-string in three months' time. A woman finished her Ph.D. thesis, which had been languishing for years, when she got a job that required its completion. To work most effectively, the deadline must be real and come from the outside. Pressure prompters tend to blow off self-created ones.

5. SCHEDULE IT IN

Before January 2004, I never exercised a day in my life. Over the past two and a half years, I have kept my resolution to exercise thirty minutes a day about 80 percent of the time. How did I do it? I put it into my day planner and treated it as an appointment with a client. Otherwise it's too easy to schedule all my time away with things I enjoy more (which is everything). Want to write every day? Block it out on your calendar. Want to start looking for a date on Match.com? Schedule it. Make a specific, time-bound appointment with yourself and you'll be much more likely to follow through.

6. DO IT DAILY

Someone asked the Dalai Lama to describe in one word the secret to living a healthy life. His answer? "Routines." Bad habits imprison us; good ones bring us closer to our heart's desire. The more you make what you want part of your everyday life, the more it will become so routine that soon you won't even have to think about it. If you want to have more work/life balance, for instance, find a way to do a little something each day: leave the office half an hour earlier, take a walk with the family after dinner, read a novel before bed.

7. MONITOR YOUR BEHAVIOR

Research shows that when you monitor your behavior in writing, you're more likely to do better. That's because monitoring is a key to self-regulation, the capacity to do what it is you say you want to. Monitoring can take the form of a food diary, counting the number of times you keep your temper in a day, logging the successes you've had with not worrying, and so forth. You also monitor yourself when you put your full attention on something—not eating and watching TV at the same time, for instance.

8. FOCUS ON THE HORIZON

Take a tip from high-performance athletes. Look at how far you've come, not how much you have left to do. Scientists call this the horizon effect. It creates encouragement ("I've done twice as much as a week ago!") and builds determination ("I've made it this far; I might as well keep going"). Focus on the ten pounds you did lose; the closet you managed to clean; the thousand-dollar debt you've wiped out; the evening you carved out for yourself. Don't forget to ask yourself how you've accomplished the task so far, so you can mine your success for ideas on how to keep going.

9. TAKE IT ONE CHOICE AT A TIME

When we think about changing something in ourselves, it can feel overwhelming. But in truth, our entire lives are constructed of the minute-by-minute choices we're making, many of which we're not even aware of. As Gary Zukav reminds us, "An unconscious choice is a reaction. . . . A conscious choice is a response." Bring your choices to consciousness. If you're having trouble sticking to your resolution for a day, try this practice: when you're doing the bad old thing, stop and say, "I'm choosing to . . ." (eat this Twinkie, not work out, stay at the office to finish this project, blow up, look at my e-mail rather than clean my desk, etc.). Do you like yourself when you make this choice? You can choose differently, moment to moment. The next day, make the positive choice visible to yourself: I'm choosing to throw this catalog away rather than go on a spending spree; I'm choosing to take a few calming breaths before speaking; I'm choosing to get my taxes done today rather than wait till April 14. The more you focus on the positive choice you can make this very day, without worrying about forever, the more you will live yourself into the new habit.

10. FIND SOMEONE WHO'S DOING WHAT YOU WANT AND IMITATE THEM

I have a friend who wants to lose weight. When we're together she says, "I'm going to watch what you eat and follow suit." When I set out to become more kind, grateful, and generous, I made a study of people I knew who had those qualities and tried to do as they did. It can be useful to read books or listen to tapes. But when it comes to changing human behavior, there's nothing that beats good old-fashioned role models. Babies learn by imitation; why shouldn't adults? Who do you know that is good at what you want to learn? What do they do that you don't? The more you intentionally watch those who are living the habit you desire, the more you have to draw on when you are by yourself. Watch and learn—and don't be afraid to ask questions: How do you get all of your work done and still have time for your family? Teach me your dating secrets. What makes you able to take risks? Most people love to teach if given the opportunity.

11. TEACH IT TO SOMEONE ELSE

A great way to really cement a new habit is to become a mentor. I was reminded of this the other day when a client of mine, who'd come to me to learn patience, said, "You'd be so proud of me, M. J. I was helping an employee of mine be more successful and I found your words about understanding when it's time to push and when it's time to hold back coming out of my mouth. I realized how much I've learned about patience, and my teaching reinforced its merits for me." One crucial tip to make this as effective as possible—whatever you suggest to someone else, practice yourself. In other words, be sure to take your own advice on the topic. It's a way to really walk the walk.

12. TREAT YOURSELF KINDLY

"Anything you know you forget. It's all about getting confused and getting unconfused." That's a piece of wisdom from Buddhist teacher Sylvia Boorstein to remind us that we're only human. We're doing the best we can. We will mess up or forget. When we do, our task is to hold ourselves in love. You and I are human beings dealing with the challenges of growth. When we treat ourselves with kindness, we don't collapse into shame or guilt but can try again with greater wisdom for having faltered.

CONSCIOUS SELF-CREATION

To exist is to change; to change is to mature; to mature is to go on creating oneself endlessly.

—HENRI BERGSON

I was reading a magazine interview with Geena Davis. She was explaining how learning archery at age forty changed her whole view of herself and ultimately led to her successful relationship of eight years after three previous divorces: "Sports are 90 percent mental," she said in *O*, "and I came to realize that there was this inner dialogue I was constantly having, where I'd be thinking, Oh that was a horrible shot, and people must be laughing at you and you should be so embarrassed. I realized that if I was telling myself that during archery, I was probably doing it all the time in the rest of my life. Becoming confident in my physical abilities, acknowledging that I had a right to take up space and be happy with my performance, was the final piece of the puzzle. . . . I began to really like myself."

Yes, I thought to myself, that's exactly how it works. You set out to do something new, like learning archery or volunteering at a soup kitchen or enjoying life more, and something bigger happens along the way. You become more aware of yourself—how you get in your own way, how you get unstuck, how you sustain momentum. And because how you do anything is how you do everything, what you learn applies not only to archery or becoming happier but to everything in your life. You now know much more about how you tick, what motivates and discourages you, and what inner qualities you have available to apply to any situation.

In interviewing the dozens of people for this book, what I was struck with over and over is how each person, like Geena Davis, not only learned a particular new habit but developed a larger reservoir of self-esteem. They felt satisfied, not only because they accomplished a particular goal but because they now knew, down to their bones, that they could do it again. This kind of self-confidence is not the kind obtained by surface affirmations, but one hewn of the sweat of lived experience. They know they can do what they set their minds to because they have.

When we set out to keep a New Year's resolution, change a habit, or bring a dream into being, ultimately we are involved in the grand act of conscious self-creation. Rather than being stuck with the way we are now, we can actually choose the habits of mind and qualities of soul we wish to cultivate. We can consciously choose the behaviors and skills we wish to learn, the life we wish to have, and follow through to a successful conclusion. Not perfectly, not always—because we all come with a load of baggage and life isn't always kind or fair—but to a much greater degree than we could before because we've had an experience of success to draw on. In these ways, creating a new habit brings us two precious spiritual gifts: hope—that our future will be brighter than today through the efforts we make—and faith—that we can bring into being more of what we desire in ourselves and in our lives. What more do we need to weave a life of meaning and beauty?

Each of us has the opportunity to change and grow until our very last breath. Happy creating.

WANT MORE SUPPORT?

Want more help to stop smoking, lose weight, find true love, get fit, get organized, or find a better job? Go to www.mj-ryan.com to sign up for guided support with these and other resolutions. You can also sign up for Daily "I Will Power" tips.

I am also available for one-on-one thinking partnerships on the phone. You can e-mail me at mjryan@mj-ryan.com.

ACKNOWLEDGMENTS

I am deeply grateful for all my angels:

My darling Ds: Don McIlraith, Dawna Markova, Daphne Rose Kingma, and, especially this time, Debra Goldstein. Don, thank you once again for your gracious willingness to take up the slack so I could write and for allowing your life to be revealed. Dawna, thank you so much for your asset focus and heartfelt generosity, particularly with practices incorporated throughout the book. Daphne, thank you for your heartful spirit. Debra, a million thank-yous for the concept and title, and the ideas and editing, especially during your move. This time I really could not have done it without you.

Sue Bender, thank you for Japanese lunches and your insights on the process.

"Broadway bombshells" Kris Puopolo, Laura Pillar, Catherine Pollock, and Brianne Ramagosa, thank you for all the behind-the-scenes work you do to make it happen.

Patrick Burke, thank you for sharing your wisdom and experience on how to make changes.

Susie Kohl, thank you for your enthusiasm and for taking up the idea as if it were your own.

Angie McArthur, thank you for graphical thinking and website conceptualization and design.

Ana Li McIlraith, thank you for putting up with my weekend absences and letting me share your stories with the world.

Barb Parmet, thank you for being such a model of change.

Pamela Peeke, thank you for Plans A–Z and for possibilities.

Robin Rankin, thank you for connecting me to some great stories.

Stephanie Ryan, thank you for sharing this life with me no matter what.

Greg Schmidt, thank you for website creation and mastering.

Linda Stone, thank you for the Hickes and for oh so many opportunities. You are one of my greatest allies.

Liz, Robert, and Nicki Taylor, thank you for babysitting help.

To my clients, some of whom appear in disguised form in these pages, and to strangers who answered my call for stories: thank you for sharing your journeys of transformation with me.

Thanks also to all the authors whose books I've cited. Their insights have broadened and deepened my thinking on this challenging topic. May the wisdom and knowledge I've collected and pulled through my own experience be of benefit.

INDEX OF TIPS AND INSPIRATIONS
BY TOPIC

INDEX